GUIDE THROUGH THE VISUDDHIMAGGA

by

U Dhammaratana

Buddhist Publication Society
P.O. Box 61
54, Sangharaja Mawatha
Kandy, Sri Lanka

First Edition, 1964, Varanasi
Second Edition, 2011, Kandy

National Library and Documentation Centre -
Cataloguing-in-Publication (CIP) Data

Dhammaratana, U.
Guide Through the Visuddhimagga / U Dhammaratana.-
Kandy: Buddhist Publication Society Inc, 2010
118p.; 22cm. - (BP 622)

ISBN 978-955-24-0357-6

i. 294.3824 DDC 22 ii. Title
1. Abhidhammapitaka

ISBN 978-955-24-0357-6

Typeset at the BPS in Charter BPS

Printed by

Ruchira Offset Printers
Kandy—Sri Lanka

CONTENTS

INTRODUCTION

Meditation may be said to be the core of Buddhism. Therefore, from the very beginning it formed an essential part of the Buddhist way of life. Various methods of meditation have been indicated in the discourses of the Buddha and his disciples. The tradition of meditation practices was handed down from teacher to pupil through the ages. There is reason to believe that later on manuals on meditation came to be written for the guidance of students. We have such a manual in the form of the *Vimuttimagga*. The original having been lost, only the Chinese translation of the whole work is now extant. An English translation of this work, called *The Path of Freedom,* has been made available through the joint efforts of a Japanese scholar and two Sinhalese monks.[1]

The *Vimuttimagga* existed before the *Visuddhimagga*. It has been ascribed to Upatissa Thera. In the beginning its authority was accepted by the Saṅgha of Sri Lanka as a whole. Later on, the members of the Mahāvihāra came to accept certain views introduced by Buddhaghosācariya as more authoritative. As a result, the *Visuddhimagga* became popular with them. However the members of the Abhayagirivihāra continued to accept the authority of the *Vimuttimagga*.

It is not only possible but also probable that Buddhaghosācariya closely followed the general plan of the *Vimuttimagga* in his own work. It would not be far from the truth to say that he expanded on the work that was already in existence, introducing his own opinions here and there.

In dealing with a certain topic Buddhaghosācariya quoted almost all the relevant facts from various sources of the canonical literature. In fact, he usually tried to be exhaustive. As a result his work was more scholarly than the *Vimuttimagga*. In the course of time, for several reasons, the former replaced the latter.

As mentioned above, meditation is an essential part of the Buddhist way of life and meditation practices cannot be explained

---

1. *The Path of Freedom,* by Ehara, Kheminda and Soma, Colombo, 1961; reprinted by BPS, Kandy, 1977, 1995.

apart from the fundamental doctrines of Buddhism. In course of his explanations, Buddhaghosācariya took full opportunity to give elaborate expositions of these fundamental doctrines. As such his work has served not only as a manual of meditation but also as the standard work on the Theravada Buddhism as a whole. No other school of Buddhism has handed down to us a work of such importance. Therefore it is no exaggeration to say that the *Visuddhi-magga*, the masterpiece of Buddhaghosācariya, occupies a unique position in the field of Buddhism in particular and the religious literature of the world in general.

What is to the advantage of the scholar is sometimes to the disadvantage of the layman. To some extent this is true of the *Visuddhi-magga*. While going through the elaborate explanations of a certain topic in the text, one is liable to lose its thread and become confused. So at times in the midst of a topic, one has to pause and relocate the thread again. This has been the experience of the author. When he came to teaching the text, he observed it was the same case for his students too, and I found it advantageous to give initially an outline of the system with reference to the essential points. In the light of the same, the details can be understood without much difficulty. It is with this object in view that the following pages have been written to serve as a guide through the *Visuddhimagga*.

In many of the Suttantas the noble path has been explained in terms of the three-fold training (*tisso sikkhā*) of virtue (*sīla*), concentration (*samādhi*) and wisdom (*paññā*). In some, such as the Rathavinīta-sutta, it has also been explained in terms of the seven purifications (*satta visuddhiyo*): (1) purification of virtue (*sīla-visuddhi*), (2) purification of mind (*citta-visuddhi*), (3) purification of views (*diṭṭhi–visuddhi*), (4) purification of overcoming of doubts (*kaṅkhāvitaraṇa-visuddhi*), (5) purification of knowledge and insight into the right and wrong path (*maggāmagga-ñāṇadassana-visuddhi*), (6) purification of knowledge and insight into practice (*paṭipadā-ñāṇa-dassana-visuddhi*), and (7) purification of knowledge and insight into the noble path (*ñāṇadassana-visuddhi*). Here it has to be noted that the first and the second purifications are represented by virtue (*sīla*) and concentration (*samādhi*), and the last five by wisdom (*paññā*). Both the *Vimuttimagga* and the *Visuddhimagga* have given their expositions of the subject-matter according to the above two methods.

The *Visuddhimagga* presents the subject-matter in 23 chapters. Among them the first two chapters are devoted to virtue and the ascetic practices (*dhutaṅga*), the next eleven chapters to concentration, and the last ten chapters to wisdom.

The present study is in three chapters. The substance of the first two chapters of the *Visuddhimagga* is given in the first chapter of our study, that of the next eleven chapters is given in the second chapter, and that of the last ten chapters is given in the third chapter.

The first chapter is in two sections giving the substance of virtue and ascetic practices (*dhutaṅga*) respectively. The second is in three sections dealing with the general principles of concentration-meditation (*samādhi*), the forty subjects of concentration-meditation (*kammaṭṭhāna*), and the benefits of the practice of the same as explained in the respective relevant chapters. Thus these two chapters are on the first two purifications.

The third chapter is in two sections. The first section refers to the general explanation of wisdom or *paññā* as given in the relevant chapters of the text, and the second refers to the remaining five kinds of purifications or *visuddhi*. Thus we have in a nutshell the essential points of *Visuddhimagga* according to both the threefold training and the seven-fold purification.

A few topics in the third and fourth chapters of the *Visuddhimagga* have been re-arranged in keeping with our method of treatment. Also, the substance of the eleventh chapter has been given before that of the tenth chapter so as to present the 36 meditation subjects connected to the (fine-) material sphere (*rūpa-kammaṭṭhāna*) together. Except for these, there are no other changes in the order of the chapters or their topics.

At the beginning of the chapters, and also certain sections, a general survey of the topics has been given. At several places certain facts have been repeated in order to present them in their logical order.

There are two English translations of the *Visuddhimagga*—one by U Pe Tin and the other by Ñāṇamoli Thera.[2] We have closely followed them in choosing the terminology of the technical terms.

If this small work is helpful, even in some measure, to students in understanding the essential points of the subject-matter, we shall feel highly rewarded.

U Dhammaratana
Nālandā

---

2. U Pe Tin, *The Path of Purity*, London, 1922. Bhikkhu Ñāṇamoli, *The Path of Purification*, BPS Kandy, 2010.

Abbreviations

AN	Aṅguttara-Nikāya
Dhp-a	*Dhammapada-Aṭṭhakathā*
M-a	*Majjhimanikāya-Aṭṭhakathā*
MN	Majjhima-Nikāya
MP	*Milindapañhā*
Nidd	Niddesa
Paṭis	Paṭisambhidāmagga
SN	Saṃyutta-Nikāya
Vin I	Vinaya Mahāvagga
Vin II	Cullavagga
Vin III	Vinaya Pācittiya
Vin V	Vinaya Parivāra

CHAPTER I

VIRTUE (*Sīla*)

SECTION I

VISM I

(1) Purification of Virtue (*Sīla-visuddhi*)

Sīla is moral discipline or virtue. It is observed in the right conduct of a person, and moral precepts have been laid down to this end. These moral precepts of Buddhism can be classified into three categories—those for the laity, those for the novices, and those for the bhikkhus, the ordained members of the Monastic Order or Saṅgha. The laity is expected to observe what are known as the five precepts (*pañca sīlāni*) in their day-to-day life. They may also observe the eight precepts on special occasions, such as full-moon-days and new-moon-days. The ten precepts are meant for the novices. For the bhikkhus, there are 227 rules in their code of discipline called the *Pātimokkha*. In the Vinaya, the canonical collection of texts dealing with monastic discipline, the reasons and implications of these rules have been worked out in some detail.

It is a matter of history that emphasis on literal conformity to rules, in the long run, leads to formalism and casuistry, overshadowing the original spirit of a discipline. Therefore it is necessary that from time to time the essential points of a discipline should be ascertained and kept in view.

The conduct of a person reflects the spirit of the moral precepts observed. The conduct expresses itself through what are known as the three doors of action (*kamma-dvārāni*)—body, speech and mind. The actions may be unwholesome (*akusala*) or wholesome (*kusala*). The unwholesome bodily actions are three-fold—killing, stealing and adultery. The verbal actions are four-fold: lying, back-biting, speaking harsh words, and gossiping. The mental actions are also three-fold—avarice, ill-will and false views. Technically they are known as the ten courses of unwholesome action (*dasa akusala-kammapathā*). The ten courses of wholesome action (*dasa kusala-kammapathā*) are represented by the abstinence from the same. These are the criteria, so to say, of ascertaining the essential nature of the moral precepts.

In a restricted sense, *sīla* has a reference to bodily and verbal actions alone. It is only in a wider sense that mental actions can be included within the definition of *sīla*. In the *sīla-samādhi-paññā*-formula, *sīla* is always used in this restricted sense.

In the codes of discipline there are certain rules which have a direct bearing on the social behaviour of a man, and there are others which have their bearing on his moral conduct alone. Keeping in view these two sets of rules, in the Buddhist tradition a distinction has been made between virtue of good behaviour (*ābhisamācārika-sīla*) and that of the beginning of a life of purity (*ādibrahmacariyaka-sīla*). One is related to the social behaviour and etiquette, while the other is related to the moral conduct. It is the observance of the latter that keeps the moral purity of a man.

The tradition speaks of many kinds of virtue. In the *Visuddhimagga*, Buddhaghosācariya has presented them in five classifications with many divisions and groups. These divisions are not exclusive. Therefore in certain cases, the same virtue occurs in several divisions. While there is an explanation of each group, the four groups representing the four-fold virtue of purification (*pārisuddhi-sīlāni*) have been explained at great length. The reason is that they cover the essential points of the monastic discipline.

In the text, Buddhaghosācariya has dealt with the topic of virtue in the form of questions and answers. It is explained under seven headings: (i) What is virtue? (ii) In what sense is it virtue? (iii) What are its characteristic (*lakkhaṇa*), function (*rasa*), manifestation (*paccupaṭṭhāna*), and proximate cause (*padaṭṭhāna*)? (iv) What are the benefits (*ānisaṃsa*) of virtue? (v) How many kinds of virtue are there? (vi) What is the defiling (*saṅkilesa*) of it? and (vii) What is the cleansing (*vodāna*) of it?

(i) What is virtue? The meaning of virtue has been interpreted in a four-fold way. The first refers to volition (*cetanā*) that functions when the observance of moral precepts is undertaken, or the religious duties are fulfilled. The second refers to the bare fact of abstinence (*virati*), represented by a mental factor. The

third refers to self-restraint (*saṃvara*), exercised through the observance of the rules of discipline (*pātimokkha-saṃvara*), mindfulness (*sati-saṃvara*), knowledge (*ñāṇa-saṃvara*), patience (*khanti-saṃvara*), and energy (*viriya-saṃvara*). The fourth refers to the non-transgression (*avītikkama*) of the moral precepts whose observance has been undertaken. The four interpretations refer to four different aspects of one and the same fact.

(ii) In what sense is it virtue? Virtue is so-called because it maintains order among the actions of a person through moral discipline, or it forms the basis of the wholesome states.

(iii) What are its characteristic, function, manifestation, and proximate cause?

(1) The characteristic of virtue is order or composition (*sīlana*). Though virtue can be presented in several ways in terms of volition, abstinence, and so on, this characteristic is common to them all. For instance, *rūpa* is of many kinds, such as blue, yellow, short, long, and so on. Though it is manifold according to colours and shapes, there is one characteristic, i.e., visibility, which is common to them all. In the same way, though virtue is manifold, the characteristic of order or composition is common to them all. It is maintained through the regulation of bodily, verbal and mental actions. It is this kind of regulation of actions that keeps order within both an individual and the society at large.

(2) The function of virtue is two-fold. In the first place, it destroys misconduct (*dussīlya*); in the second place, it keeps a person innocent (*anavajja*). Therefore virtue has two aspects—a negative one and a positive one.

(3) The appearance of virtue is purity (*soceyya*). We know a man by his appearance. In the same way, we know virtue by purity—its appearance. This purity is three-fold—purity of bodily actions (*kāya-soceyya*), purity of verbal actions (*vacī-soceyya*), and purity of mental actions (*mano-soceyya*).

(4) The proximate cause refers to the immediate reason that conditions the cultivation of virtue. It is two-fold—conscience (*ottappa*) and shame (*hiri*). A person does not commit misdeeds either because he is governed by the dictates

of his conscience, or because he has consideration for the public opinion. If he were to commit a misdeed, in the first place, he would suffer the pricks of conscience, and in the second place he would be subject to public censure and even corporal punishment according to the seriousness of the case. For the same reason, conscience and shame have been characterised as the two primary conditions which maintain law and order in the world (*loka-pālaka-dhamma*). If not for them, there would be chaos and confusion not only in the individuals but also in the society at large.

(iv) What are the benefits of virtue? As regards the benefits of virtue, in the discourses of the Master many of them have been mentioned. Non-remorse (*avippaṭisāra*) has been mentioned as one of its great benefits. A mind free from repentance is full of tranquillity. Such a mind easily attains concentration (*samādhi*). On one occasion addressing Ānanda, the Master remarked, "Ānanda! Virtues have non-remorse as their aim and benefit" (A IV 99). On another occasion, as reported in the Mahāparinibbānasutta, speaking on the same topic to a gathering of lay devotees at Pāṭaliputta, the Master referred to the following five benefits of virtue: a virtuous man would come into possession of a large fortune as a result of his diligence; his name and fame would spread; he would attend an assembly without any kind of fear or hesitation as he has no charges against him; he would die with an easy conscience; and he would be born in a happy place after death (D II 69–70). On still another occasion, addressing the disciples the Master said, "If a bhikkhu should wish to be loved and respected by the fellow-brethren, he should lead a virtuous life" (M I 44). These are some of the benefits referred to by the Buddha himself. Virtue is the very foundation of a life of righteousness. The dirt of defilements, not to be cleansed even by the waters of the five great rivers—Gaṅgā, Yamunā, Aciravatī, Sarabhū and Mahī—can be washed away by virtue alone. The soothing effect of sandalwood, pearls, moon-beams and so on is no remedy for the burning sensations created by passions. Cessation of such sensations can be brought about only through the soothing effect of virtue. The fragrance of flowers and other things would be wafted only in the direction of the wind, but the fragrance of virtue would be wafted all round. Virtue is the ladder that leads to heaven. The ultimate purpose of the cultivation of virtue is the attainment of Nibbāna. For the same reason, it has also been characterised as the entrance to the city of Nibbāna.

(v) How many kinds of virtue are there? In the *Visuddhimagga,* different kinds of virtue have been classified in numerical order from one to five.

(1) All virtues are said to be of one kind in so far as they serve one and the same purpose of leading to self-composition. As such there is only one division and one group in the first classification.

(2) In the second classification there are seven divisions of two groups each:

(a) Virtue of keeping (*cāritta-sīla*) and that of avoiding (*vāritta-sīla*). Performing what the Master has recommended is the virtue of keeping, and not committing what the Master has prohibited is the virtue of avoiding.

(b) Virtue of good behaviour (*ābhisamācārika-sīla*) and that of the beginning of the life of purity (*ādibrahmacariyaka-sīla*). One is the fulfilment of the small duties of the monastic life. The other is the observance of the moral precepts, which leads to the attainment of the higher states. The latter is so called because it constitutes the basis of the religious life.

(c) Virtue of abstinence (*virati-sīla*) and that of non abstinence (*avirati-sīla*). The first refers to abstinence from killing, etc. The other refers to volition, etc.

(d) Dependent virtue (*nissita-sīla*) and independent virtue (*anissita-sīla*). The first refers to virtue based on (i) desire or (ii) a false view. Thus virtue observed with a view to be born in heaven belongs to virtue based on desire, and virtue treated as an end in itself belongs to virtue based on false view. When virtue is not affected by either desire and false view, it is said to be independent.

(e) Temporary virtue (*kālapariyanta-sīla*) and lifelong virtue (*āpāṇakoṭika-sīla*). The first refers to virtue observed only for a limited period, whereas the second refers to that observed up to the end of life.

(f) Limited virtue (*sapariyanta-sīla*) and unlimited virtue (*apariyanta-sīla*). The first refers to virtue that is violated in the interest of gain, fame, relatives, limbs and life. The second refers to virtue that is observed even at the cost of all this.

(g) Mundane virtue (*lokiya-sīla*) and supramundane virtue (*lokuttara-sīla*). The first refers to virtue that is defiled (*sāsava*) and the second refers to virtue that is free from all defilements (*anāsava*).

(3) In the third classification there are five divisions of three groups each:

(a) Inferior virtue (*hīna-sīla*), medium virtue (*majjhima-sīla*) and superior virtue (*paṇīta-sīla*). Virtue undertaken out of desire for fame, etc., is inferior, that undertaken for the sake of merit is medium, and that undertaken in consideration of the noble nature of the practice itself is superior. Several other explanations have also been given.

(b) Virtue giving precedence to self (*attādhipateyya-sīla*), that giving precedence to the world (*lokādhipateyya sīla*), and that giving precedence to Dhamma (*dhammādhipateyya-sīla*). The first refers to virtue observed out of regard for one's position, the second refers to that observed out of consideration for the public opinion, and the third refers to that observed out of respect for Dhamma.

(c) Affected virtue (*parāmaṭṭha-sīla*), not-affected virtue (*aparāmaṭṭha-sīla*) and tranquillised virtue (*paṭippassaddhi-sīla*). The first refers to virtue affected by desire and false view, the second refers to virtue not so affected, and the third refers to virtue of the Arahants. It is so called because since an Arahant has fulfilled virtue, his exertion has come to an end.

(d) Purified virtue (*visuddha-sīla*), unpurified virtue (*avisuddha-sīla*), and dubious virtue (*vematika-sīla*). The first refers to virtue observed without committing any offence, or in case of commission, proper amends have been made. The second refers to a case where an offence has been committed, but no amends have been made. The third refers to a case where one is in doubt as to whether an offence has been committed or not, and where an offence has been committed, one is in doubt regarding its nature.

(e) Virtue of the learner (*sekha-sīla*), that of the non-learner (*asekha-sīla*), and that of neither (*nevasekha-nāsekha-sīla*). The first refers to virtue of those who have attained the first seven supramundane states, the second refers to that of the Arahants, and the third refers to that of a worldling.

(4) In the fourth classification there are four divisions of four groups each:

(a) Virtue partaking of diminution (*hānabhāgiya-sīla*), of stagnation (*ṭhitibhāgiya-sīla*), of distinction (*visesa-bhāgiya-sīla*), and of penetration (*nibbedhabhāgiya-sīla*). The first refers to virtue of a person who has fallen from a position of virtue due to negligence, the second refers to virtue of a person who remains where he is, the third refers to virtue of a person who makes further progress in religious life on the basis of his virtue, and the fourth refers to the virtue of a person who is able to develop insight-knowledge into the true nature of things.

(b) Virtue of ordained monks (*bhikkhu-sīla*), of ordained nuns (*bhikkhunī-sīla*), of novices (*anupasampanna-sīla*), and of the laity (*gahaṭṭha-sīla*). They refer to the precepts to be observed by the four categories of the disciples of the Buddha.

(c) Natural virtue (*pakati-sīla*), customary virtue (*ācāra-sīla*), necessary virtue (*dhammatā-sīla*), and virtue related to previous experience (*pubba-hetuka-sīla*). The first refers to virtue observed by beings of certain planes as a matter of course, the second refers to observance of customs prevalent in a particular society, the third refers to virtues of an extra-ordinary nature that do not come within the normal state of affairs, and the fourth refers to the noble virtues of great beings conditioned by their experience in previous births.

(d) Virtue of restraint of the code of discipline (*pātimokkha-saṃvara-sīla*), of restraint of sense-faculties (*indriya-saṃvara-sīla*), of purification of livelihood (*ājīva-pārisuddhi-sīla*), and of basic requisites (*paccaya-sannissita-sīla*). Great importance has been attached to these four groups, which have a special application to the bhikkhus. Therefore their explanation will be given here at some length.

(i) The virtue of restraint of the code of discipline. It is fulfilled by leading a disciplined life according to the rules of the Vinaya. The meditator who leads such a life conducts himself properly both in private and public life (*ācāra-sampanno*). He keeps the company of such persons and frequents such places as would be conducive to his way of life, and avoids the company of persons and the frequenting of places of the opposite nature (*gocara-sampanno*). Further he sees danger even in the violation of minor rules of discipline, such as those related to matters of etiquette (*anumattesu vajjesu bhaya-dassāvī*).

(ii) The virtue of the restraint of sense-faculties. It is fulfilled by exercising control over the sense organs. We receive information about the world through the sense-organs. For instance, we perceive the world as represented by visual objects (*rūpāyatana*) with the eye. This is true of the other sense-objects and their respective sense-organs also. Now the controlling of the sense-organs does not mean non-perception of their objects. It means to perceive the objects in their true nature, without taking a superficial and hence a perverted view which could give rise to defilements, such as passion, hate and so on. In the beginning this can be done by cultivating mindfulness. This point has to be understood with reference to the explanation given in the Abhidhamma. According to the Abhidhamma a full course of cognition that arises in relation to the first five sense-organs is represented by sixteen thought-moments beginning with vibration in the life-continuum (*bhavaṅga-calana*) and ending with registering consciousness (*tadālambana*). The course of cognition related to the mind-door (*manodvāra*) is represented by 10 thought moments. In the case of the first five courses of cognition, the thought-moments from life-continuum to determining (*voṭṭhapana*) are concerned only with the perception of the respective objects. Therefore they may be said to be more or less passive in nature. It is at the next stage, called impulsive activity or *javana,* which is usually represented by seven thought-moments, that the mind becomes active. At this stage it takes a decision and passes judgement on the object. If it is an unpleasant one, it will give rise to the unwholesome mental states (*akusala-dhamma*), such as passion, hate, etc. Therefore it is the *javana* stage of mind that has to be taken care of. In fact it is the point of control. When it is controlled the sense-organ concerned is said to be well-guarded. This has been explained with reference to the analogy of a well-fortified city, whose entrance is well-guarded. For this reason, with reference to the controlling of the eye it has been said: when the meditator sees a visual object, he does not take a superficial view of it as a whole (*na nimittaggāhī hoti*), nor does he take a superficial view of different parts of it individually (*nānubyañjanaggāhī hoti*), which could lead to the arising of greed, hate, etc. This is true of the remaining sense organs also.[1]

(iii) The virtue of the purity of livelihood. Food and certain other things are necessary to maintain life. Even a meditator whose goal is Nibbāna has to depend on

1. M I 231.

these basic necessities of life. He has to obtain them by right means. In this connection the *Visuddhimagga* refers to six rules of the Parivāra of the Vinaya, specially related to the subject-matter.[2] The meditator is not to seek his necessities by resorting to the following objectionable methods: hypocrisy (*kuhanā*), flattering (*lapanā*), hinting (*nemittikatā*), belittling virtues of others and magnifying one's own virtues (*nippesikatā*), and giving something to others with a view to get more or something better in return (*lābhena lābhaṃ nijigīsanatā*). Further it also instructs the meditator not to take to such professional practices as astrology, dream-interpretation and so on, which have been mentioned in the Brahmajāla-sutta.[3]

(iv) The virtue of the proper use of the basic requisites. It is fulfilled by making the right use of the basic requisites got by right means. This has to be done by keeping in mind the purpose of their use. The basic requisites are four-fold: robe (*cīvara*), alms-food (*piṇḍapāta*), residence (*senāsana*) and medicine (*gilānapaccaya*). The robe is the first requisite. It is meant to cover up the nakedness of the body, and protect it against climatic extremes and the bites of mosquitoes and creeping things, so that the meditator can lead a life free from discomfort and danger and fulfil the mission of his life. The robe is not meant for beautifying the body. Alms-food is the second requisite. In using it the meditator has to remember that it is meant for maintaining life, so that the noble life may be led. It is not meant for building up a good physique as done by the physical culturists. Residence is the third requisite. In using it the meditator has to bear in mind that it is meant to protect him against the inclement weather and other dangers to life and virtue. Medicine is the fourth requisite. In using it also he has to remember its utility.

---

2. Vin V 146.
3. D I 10.

(5) In the fifth classification, there are two divisions of five groups each:

(i) Virtue of limited purification (*pariyanta-pārisuddhi-sīla*), of unlimited purification (*apariyanta-pārisuddhi-sīla*), of fulfilled purification (*paripuṇṇa-pārisuddhi-sīla*), of unadhered-to purification (*aparāmaṭṭha-pārisuddhi-sīla*), and of tranquillised purification (*paṭippassaddhi-pārisuddhi-sīla*). The first refers to precepts other than those of the bhikkhus, the second refers to the precepts of the ordained members of the Monastic Order, the third refers to the virtue of the good worldling, the fourth refers to the virtue of the noble ones who have attained the first seven supramundane states, and the fifth refers to the virtue of the Arahants.

(ii) Virtue of abandoning (*pahāna-sīla*), of refraining (*veramaṇī-sīla*), of volition (*cetanā-sīla*), of restraint (*saṃvara-sīla*), and of non-transgression (*avītikkama-sīla*). The *Visuddhimagga* quotes in full the detailed explanation of these virtues as given in the Paṭisambhidāmagga.[4] They have been explained with reference to the ten courses of unwholesome action, the unwholesome states overcome in trances, the misconceptions removed by developing the eighteen kinds of principal insights (*aṭṭhārasa mahāvipassanā*), and the fetters destroyed by the supramundane paths. The fulfilment of this five-fold virtue has been explained with reference to all the relevant states one by one; for instance, with reference to the first course of unwholesome action (*akusala-kamma-patha*), it is said—in case of killing a living thing (*pāṇātipāta*), abandoning is virtue, abstinence is virtue, volition is virtue, restraint is virtue, and non-transgression is virtue. Thus each case has been explained with reference to all the five aspects of *sīla*.

(vi) What is the defiling of it? Virtue is said to be defiled when the precepts are violated. This violation may be of a minor or a

4. Paṭis 47–53.

major nature. Whatever it is, it is the temptations that are at the root of all the violations.

(vii) What is the cleansing of it? Virtue is said to be pure when the precepts are observed without any violation. This can be done in two ways: by realising the dangers of their violation, and through the benefits of keeping them. These two ways have been explained with reference to quotations given from several suttantas.

In the light of these instructions, when the meditator goes on fulfilling virtues, he becomes free from so many unwholesome states. As a result, his mind becomes serene and tends towards concentration (*samādhi*).

SECTION II
Vism II

Practices of Purification (Dhutaṅga)

Dhutaṅga are practices of purification. They are so called because their observance leads to a life of purity. Therefore they have been characterised as observances or practices which have a bearing on the religious life (*vata*). *Dhutaṅga* are not virtue (*sīla*) as such. For this reason they were not included in the chapter on virtue but were treated in a separate chapter of their own. However, as they are closely related to virtue, they are dealt with immediately after the former.

References in Early Literature

No mention was made of *dhutaṅga* as such in the Suttas and in the Vinaya. Certain ascetic practices included among *dhutaṅga* were mentioned individually in several suttantas. Among others, we come across the following words—*sapadāhacārī, piṇḍapātika, paṃsukulika, abbhokāsika, āraññika* and *pantasenāsanika*. In the Saṃyutta-Nikāya[5] and the Etadaggapāli of the Aṅguttara-Nikāya,[6] Mahākassapa Thera, one of the eighty principal disciples of the Master, has

5. S II 132.
6. A I 23.

been described as the foremost among those who teach *dhutas*. The Niddesa refers to eight *dhutaṅga*.[7] In the *Milindapañhā*, a late work, 13 *dhutaṅga* are listed together for the first time.[8]

Both the *Visuddhimagga* and the *Vimuttimagga* give ful explanations of these practices.

Dhutaṅga and the Middle Path

To some extent *dhutaṅga* can be said to be ascetic practices. So sometimes the question is asked as to how could their position be reconciled with the Middle Path of the Buddha. In this connection it has to be noted that the Buddha did not prescribe *dhutaṅga* as compulsory practices to be observed by one and all. In the beginning, the four basic requisites (*nissaya*) were made compulsory for all the bhikkhus.[9] But later on, they had to be relaxed in consideration of the practical necessities. They became optional practices to be observed by those who found them conducive to their religious life.

There is reason to believe that the Buddha recognised the existence of what may be called the ascetic temperament. He permitted monks with such a temperament to observe these practices. But he did not want to attach undue importance to external practices. Here again, he wanted his disciples not to give any publicity to them for the sake of name, fame and gain. One was expected to observe them even without the knowledge of one's fellow-brethren.

It is on record that once Devadatta went to the Buddha and requested him to make the following five rigorous practices compulsory for the bhikkhus: they should remain all their life in the forest, live under trees, live on alms only, use robes made of rags only, and be pure vegetarians (Vin II 197).

The Buddha refused to grant his request. He said that those who wished to follow these practices may do so, but they would not

---

7. Nidd I 66.
8. Mil 359.
9. The four *nissaya* refer to the minimum requisites prescribed for bhikkhus: 1. To live on food received by begging only (*piṇḍapātikaṅga*), 2. To use robes made of rags only (*paṃsukūlikaṅga*), 3. To live at the foot of a tree (*rukkhamūlikaṅga*), and 4. To use only myrobalans fermented in cow urine as medicine (*pūtimutta-bhesajja*). See Vin I 58, 96. Cf. A II 26.

be made compulsory for all. This also shows that he did not want to attach undue importance to them.

It is quite clear from the first sermon and several other discourses that the Buddha rejected self-mortification (*attakilamathānuyoga*) as such. He even declared ascetic practices as obstacles to a higher life. When it is said that the Buddha rejected asceticism, it does not mean that he encouraged self-indulgence (*kāmasukhallikānuyoga*), the other extreme. He rejected it with the same deprecation.

What the Buddha wanted was that the people should lead a decent life and not a shabby one, a healthy life of simple habits and not a life of luxury, and cultivate the noble virtues. He believed in a healthy mind in a healthy body. While he rejected asceticism as a creed, he believed in strict moral discipline.

According to Mahāsakuludāyi-sutta (MN 77), when Udāyi, an ascetic, told the Buddha that the latter was venerated by the people for his life of holiness, purity and simplicity, the Buddha remarked that in the matter of simplicity there were his own disciples who surpassed him. For instance, there was Mahākassapa who observed rigorous practices. He lived all his life on alms, begged from door to door, and spent his days in the forest, whereas the Buddha used to live occasionally in palatial buildings and accept royal invitations.

He further said in reply to Udāyi that the wise men paid homage to the Tathāgata for his attainments in higher culture (*adhisīla*), knowledge and vision (*ñāṇadassana*), higher wisdom (*adhipaññā*), and above all for that liberation of mind which is not to be perturbed again (*akuppā-cetovimutti*). From all this we can have some idea about the attitude of the Buddha regarding *dhutaṅga*.

It is from the point of view of simplicity that the Buddha must have permitted the practice of *dhutaṅga*. There is enough evidence to show that during the lifetime of the Master, some of his disciples observed these rigorous practices. Later on, they became popular with a section of the Saṅgha. That tradition was handed down from generation to generation. At present the *dhutaṅga* are observed only by the bhikkhus who live in forest hermitages. There are thirteen *dhutaṅga*:

(i) The practice of wearing robes made out of rags (*paṃsukūlikaṅga*), collected from streets, cemeteries, etc.

(ii) The practice of having only three robes (*tecīvarikaṅga*). The three robes are the outer double robe (*saṅghāṭi*), outer robe (*uttarāsaṅga*) and inner robe (*antaravāsaka*).

(iii) The practice of living on alms collected from door to door (*piṇḍapātikaṅga*). In observing this practice the meditator has to give up the fourteen kinds of food-offering permitted in the Vinaya such as partaking in a meal offered to the Order.

(iv) The practice of begging from house to house in consecutive order (*sapadānacārikaṅga*), without leaving any house in-between on considerations of wealth, position, etc.

(v) The practice of taking meals at one sitting (*ekāsanikaṅga*), without interruption. Once the meal is discontinued, it is not to be resumed.

(vi) The practice of having only one bowl in which all kinds of food have to be taken (*pattapiṇḍikaṅga*). No other plate or saucer can be used for the purpose.

(vii) The practice of not taking any food after finishing or after expressing the intention of finishing one's meal (*khalupacchābhattikaṅga*).

(viii) The practice of dwelling only in forests (*āraññikaṅga*), which should be at a considerable distance from human habitation.

(ix) The practice of living under a tree (*rukkhamūlikaṅga*). Such a tree must not be one of the boundary marks of a village, or one within the compound of a monastery or a shrine, or a fruit-bearing tree.

(x) The practice of living in the open (*abbhokāsikaṅga*). One observing this *dhutaṅga* and the practice of living under a tree (*rukkhamūlikaṅga*) is permitted to take shelter in a covered place at the time of raining.

(xi) The practice of living in a cemetery (*sosānikaṅga*). A plot of land set apart for a cemetery, but not yet used, is not to be treated as a cemetery (*susāna*). One left unused by the people even for twelve years, after using it even once, is to be treated as a cemetery.

(xii) The practice of using whatever bed or seat is allotted to one without any change (*yathāsanthatikaṅga*).

(xiii) The practice of spending nights in the sitting posture without lying down (*nesajjikaṅga*). A meditator practising this *dhutaṅga* can use other postures (*iriyapātha*) also.

The Meaning of the Term *Dhutaṅga*

The meaning of the term *dhutaṅga*, lit. "factor for shaking off (defilements)," has been interpreted in three ways: In the first place, these practices are called *dhutaṅga* because they are observed by one who is given to shaking off the defilements. In the second place, they are so called because the knowledge of shaking off, which shakes off defilements, forms part of these practices. In the third place, they are so called because they constitute the path that leads to the shaking off of the defilements.

Dhutaṅga Explained Under Five Matrices

All the *dhutaṅga* have each been explained under five matrices or lists (*mātikā*): (i) method of undertaking (*samādāna*), (ii) directions and conditions (*vidhāna*), (iii) grades (*pabheda*), (iv) breach (*bheda*) and (v) benefit (*ānisaṃsa*).

(i) The first matrix explains how the meditator has to undertake the observance of a *dhutaṅga*. In each case two statements have been given. The meditator has to undertake it with reference to one of them. For instance, in the case of *paṃsukūlikaṅga,* he has to undertake it with reference to one of the following statements: "I refuse robes given by householders" or "I undertake the refuse-rag-wearer's practice."

(ii) The second matrix gives the directions for and the conditions under which a *dhutaṅga* has to be observed. Thus in the case of the practice of wearing robes made out of rags the directions refer to the nature of rags that the meditator may pick up for making his robes.

(iii) The third matrix explains how many grades are there. In each case, three grades have been mentioned— strict (*ukkaṭṭha*), moderate (*majjhima*) and mild (*muduka*). One who is very strict in his observance is said to be strict, another who is moderate is said to be moderate, and a third who is not very strict is said to be mild.

(iv) The fourth matrix explains under what conditions the breach of a *dhutaṅga* is committed.

(v) The fifth matrix explains the benefits of observing the *dhutaṅga* practices. While each *dhutaṅga* has its own benefits, they all lead to the common benefits explained in relation to the practices of the noble lineage (*ariyavaṃsa*) Having a few necessities (*appicchatā*), contentment (*santuṭṭhitā*), effacement of defilements (*sallekhatā*), and cultivating detachment (*pavivekatā*).

How Many *Dhutaṅga* are to be Practised

A bhikkhu, an ordained member of the order of monks (*bhikkhusaṅgha*), may practise all the 13 *dhutaṅga*. Here it has to be noted that a bhikkhu who observes one or more severe *dhutaṅga* may not observe others which are less severe. Thus one who dwells in the open need not observe the practice of dwelling at the root of a tree. One who begs from house to house is necessarily one who goes on alms. One who taking meals at one sitting can easily be one who only eats out of his bowl or one who is not taking any food after finishing.

A bhikkhunī, a member of the order of nuns (*bhikkhunīsaṅgha*), is allowed to practise only eight of the thirteen *dhutaṅga*. The exceptions are: forest dwelling, not taking food after finishing, living in the open, dwelling at the root of tree, and dwelling in a cemetery. In the beginning bhikkhunīs also used to follow some of the practices such as forest-dwelling but then they were troubled by rogues, and therefore they had to be debarred from observing such practices.

A novice (*sāmaṇera*) is allowed to observe twelve *dhutaṅga*, the exception being the practice of only wearing three robes. A female trainee (*sikkhamānā*) or a female novice (*sāmaṇerī*) is allowed to observe seven of the *dhutaṅga* observed by bhikkhunīs, with again the exception being the practice of only wearing three robes. For lay-followers (*upāsaka* and *upāsikā*) only two *dhutaṅga*, namely, eating at one sitting and eating only out of a bowl, have been recommended. The remaining *dhutaṅga* are not in keeping with their way of life.

CHAPTER II

CONCENTRATION (*Samādhi*)

SECTION I
(2) Purification of Mind
(*Citta-visuddhi*)

VISM III–IV

Purification of mind (*citta-visuddhi*) or concentration (*samādhi*) is the second stage in the path of purification. It is three-fold momentary concentration (*khaṇika-samādhi*), access-concentration (*upacāra-samādhi*) and fixed-concentration (*appanā-samādhi*). The first appears intermittently in certain wholesome types of thought. The second is gained just before attaining a jhāna (absorption). For this reason it is known as neighbourhood concentration. The third is the full-fledged concentration which marks the attainment of a jhāna as such. The first is momentary in nature, the second is more durable, and the third lasts for a long time. A meditator can penetrate into the true nature of things even with reference to the first type of concentration. But it can be done with greater ease at the higher levels. Therefore the latter two have an advantage over the first.

Samādhi or concentration has been used in a general sense for concentration that is associated with all types of thought—moral, immoral and non-moral. For the same reason, in the Abhidhamma it has been included among those mental factors which are common to all types of thought (*sabbacittasādhāraṇa-cetasikāni*). But it has to be noted that there is a great difference between concentration associated with the lower types of thought and that associated with the higher ones. In the latter the mind gets absorbed in the object, whereas in the former it becomes aloof from it. Therefore this difference amounts not to one of degree but to one of kind.

Buddhaghosācariya deals with this topic in eleven chapters (Chs. 3 to 13), covering 323 pages in the PTS edition. He explains concentration under eight matrices (*mātikā*). The first six matrices are explained in 4 pages. The explanation of the seventh matrix covers some 287 pages. The last and the eighth matrix is explained in 36 pages.

As usual, Buddhaghosācariya is quite exhaustive. He explains not only different types of concentration, and for that matter *jhāna* (absorption) and the practices that lead to their attainment, but also gives certain instructions which the meditator has to observe to create a congenial atmosphere for the same.

The third and the fourth chapters of the text deal with the general points of the technique of development (*bhāvanā*) of concentration with special reference to the earth *kasiṇa.* The next seven chapters explain the nature of the remaining subjects of concentration. The last two chapters deal with the supernormal powers. In the present study we have treated all the eleven chapters in one under a number of sub-headings.

This topic was explained initially under eight headings in the form of eight questions: (i) What is concentration? (ii) In what sense is it concentration? (iii) What are its characteristic, function, manifestation, and proximate cause? (iv) How many kinds of concentration are there? (v) What is its defilement? (vi) What is its cleansing? (vii) How should it be developed? (viii) What are the benefits of the development of concentration?

(i) What is concentration? In the present context, concentration has been defined as the unification of the wholesome mental states (*kusala-cittekaggatā samādhi*).

(ii) In what sense is it concentration? Concentration is so called because it focuses the respective types of mind and their associating mental factors on a single object (*ekārammaṇe*).

(iii) What are its characteristic, function, manifestation, and proximate cause? Concentration has non-distraction as its characteristic. Its function is to eliminate distraction. It is manifested as non-wavering. Its proximate cause is bliss.

(iv) How many kinds of concentration are there? The different kinds of concentration have been presented in five classifications in their numerical order:

(1) All kinds of concentration have the common characteristic of concentrating the mind on a single object. For this reason, they are said to be of one kind.

(2) In the second classification there are four divisions of two groups each:

  (a) Access (*upacāra*) and fixed (*appanā*). In access-concentration the five *nivāraṇa* or hindrances are overcome. Fixed-concentration or absorption marks the full-fledged concentration. Access-concentration precedes fixed-concentration.

  (b) Mundane (*lokiya*) and supramundane (*lokuttara*). The first is associated with the wholesome types of mind of the three planes of existence, and the other is associated with those of the supramundane plane.

  (c) Associated with joy (*sappītika*) and not associated with joy (*nippītika*). The first refers to jhāna where joy exists, and the other to jhāna where it does not exist. The categorization varies according to the four-fold and the five-fold methods of classifying jhāna.

  (d) Associated with bliss (*sukhasahagata*) and associated with equanimity (*upekkhāsahagata*). One refers to the jhāna where bliss exists, and the other refers to those where it does not exist. Their categorization too varies according to the two methods.

(3) In the third classification, there are four divisions of three groups each:

  (a) Inferior (*hīna*), moderate (*majjhima*) and superior (*paṇīta*). Concentration just attained is called inferior, that which is developed to some extent is called moderate, and that which is well developed is called superior.

  (b) Associated with applied thought and sustained thought (*savitakka-savicāra*), associated with sustained thought, but not with applied thought (*avitakka-savicāra*), and not associated with applied thought or sustained thought (*avitakka-avicāra*). They have to be understood in relation to the respective jhāna. Their categorization varies according to the two methods.

(c) Associated with joy (*pītisahagata*), associated with bliss (*sukhasahagata*), and associated with equanimity (*upekkhāsahagata*). They exist in the relevant jhāna. Their categorization too varies according to the two methods.

(d) Undeveloped (*paritta*), exalted (*mahaggata*), and measureless (*appamāṇa*). Concentration associated with the access-state (*upacāra*) is said to be undeveloped as it is limited in scope, that associated with jhāna is exalted, and that associated with the supramundane states is measureless.

(4) In the fourth classification there are six divisions of four groups each:

(a) Associated with difficult practice and slow direct knowledge (*dukkhāpaṭipado dandhābhiñño*), associated with difficult practice and rapid direct knowledge (*dukkhāpaṭipado khippābhiñño*), associated with easy practice and slow direct knowledge (*sukhāpaṭipado dandhābhiñño*), and associated with easy practice and rapid direct knowledge (*sukhāpaṭipado khippābhiñño*). Here the terms "practice" (*paṭipadā*) and "direct knowledge" (*abhiñña*) have been used in a technical sense. The meditation practices from the first effort up to access-concentration are called "practice." The knowledge that functions from access-concentration up to fixed-concentration is called "direct knowledge." Now, the practice may be difficult or easy, and the attainment of direct knowledge slow or rapid. Accordingly the four alternatives are possible.

(b) Limited concentration with a limited object (*paritto parittārammaṇo*); limited concentration with an unlimited object (*paritto appamāṇārammaṇo*), unlimited concentration with a limited object (*appamāṇo parittārammaṇo*), and unlimited concentration with an unlimited object (*appamāṇo appamāṇārammaṇo*). The first refers to concentration attained on an undeveloped mental image or sign (*nimitta*), and which cannot be the basis for attaining a higher jhāna. The second refers to concentration attained on a developed sign, but cannot serve as the basis for attaining a higher jhāna. The third refers to concentration attained on an undeveloped sign, but can serve as the basis for attaining a higher jhāna. The fourth refers to concentration attained on an unlimited sign and which can also serve as the basis for attaining a higher jhāna.

(c) Associated with applied thought, sustained thought, rapture, bliss and concentration (*vitakka-vicāra pīti-sukha-samādhi-sahitaṃ*), associated with rapture, bliss and concentration (*pīti-sukha-samādhi-sahitaṃ*), associated with bliss and concentration (*sukha-samādhi-sahitaṃ*), and associated with equanimity and concentration (*upekkhā-samādhi-sahitaṃ*). In their consecutive order, they refer to the four jhānas according to the four-fold method.

(d) Concentration partaking of diminution (*hāna-bhāgiya*), concentration partaking of stagnation (*ṭhiti-bhāgiya*), concentration partaking of distinction (*visesabhāgiya*), and concentration partaking of penetration (*nibbedha-bhāgiya*). The first refers to a jhāna which may be lost due to the influence of unfavourable conditions. The second refers to a jhāna which remains steady due to the presence of favourable conditions. The third refers to a jhāna which remains not only steady, but can also be the basis for attaining the higher *jhānic* states. The fourth refers to a jhāna on the basis of which a meditator can penetrate into the true nature of things.

(e) Concentration of the sensual plane (*kāmāvacaro samādhi*), concentration of the fine-material plane (*rūpāvacaro samādhi*), concentration of the immaterial plane (*arūpāvacaro samādhi*), and concentration of the supramundane plane (*apariyāpanno samādhi*). This classification has been done according to the four planes of consciousness.

(f) Concentration attained on the basis of willpower (*chanda-samādhi*), that attained on the basis of strong endeavour (*viriya-samādhi*), that attained on the basis of mind-control (*citta-samādhi*), and that attained on the basis of investigation (*vīmaṃsa-samādhi*).

(5) In the fifth classification, concentration has been taken into consideration according to the five-fold method of classifying jhānas.

(v) What is its defilement? Concentration is said to be defiled due to the presence of unfavourable conditions which would cause the fall of the meditator from a higher state to a lower one.

(vi) What is its cleansing? Concentration is said to be purified due to the presence of favourable conditions which would help the meditator in attaining a higher state from a lower one.

(vii) How should it be developed? The explanation of this topic covers as many as two hundred pages. It is dealt with under the heading below.

(viii) What are the benefits of the development of concentration? The benefits of concentration are summarised in Section III below. Among them, the attainment of the one-pointedness of mind for penetrating into the true nature of things is the most important.

Development of Concentration

Vism III

Forty Subjects of Meditation

There are forty subjects of meditation (*kammaṭṭhāna*):

(i) Ten *kasiṇas:* earth-*kasiṇa*, water-*kasiṇa*, fire-*kasiṇa*, air-*kasiṇa*, blue-*kasiṇa*, yellow-*kasiṇa*, red-*kasiṇa*, white-*kasiṇa*, light-*kasiṇa*, and limited space-*kasiṇa*.

(ii) Ten kinds of foulness (*asubha*): the bloated state, the livid state, the festering state, the cut-up state, the gnawed state, the scattered state, the hacked and scattered state, the bleeding state, the worm-infested state, and the state of a skeleton.

(iii) The ten kinds of recollection (*anussatiyo*): recollection of the Buddha, recollection of the Dhamma, recollection of the Saṅgha, recollection of virtue, recollection of generosity, recollection of deities, mindfulness of death, mindfulness of the body, mindfulness of breathing, and recollection of peace.

(iv) The four sublime states (*brahmavihāra*): universal love (*mettā*), compassion (*karuṇā*), sympathetic joy (*mudita*), and equanimity (*upekkhā*).

(v) The four immaterial states (*āruppa*): the state of boundless space (*ākāsānañcāyatana*), the state of boundless consciousness (*viññāṇañcāyatana*), the state of nothingness (*ākiñcaññāyatana*), and the state of neither perception nor non-perception (*nevasaññānāsaññāyatana*).

(vi) One perception (*ekasaññā*).

(vii) One defining (*ekavavatthāna*).[10]

Among the forty subjects of meditation two—loving kindness and mindfulness of death—are beneficial to all under all circumstances. Loving kindness creates a peaceful atmosphere and the mindfulness of death creates an urge in the meditator to lead the religious life in all earnestness. As regards the other meditation subjects, a meditator chooses one according to his temperament.

Ten Impediments

The meditator has to give undivided attention to the meditation practices to attain good results. For this purpose he has to keep his mind entirely free from other affairs which could disturb it. In this connection Buddhaghosācariya refers to the ten impediments or *paḷibodha* found in the following verse (*gāthā*):

> A dwelling, family, and gain
> A class, and building too as fifth,
> And travel, kin, affliction, books,
> And supernormal powers: ten.[11]

(i) Dwelling place or abode (*āvāsa*) can be an obstacle if one takes an interest in its affairs, and has attachment to it. In this connection Buddhaghosācariya relates a story to show that for one who has no attachment, an abode cannot be an obstacle.

---

10. For their detailed explanation see Chapter 2, Section 2, below.
11. Translation by Bh. Ñāṇamoli, *The Path of Purification*, III. 29.

(ii) Family (*kulaṃ*) refers to the families of one's relatives and those of one's lay devotees. By too much of association with them, one is likely to develop attachment to them. Here too, the teacher relates the story of a young bhikkhu who had developed detachment to such an extent that he did not disclose himself to his parents even on visiting them after a long absence.

(iii) Gain (*lābha*): Sometimes requisites (*paccaya*) become a source of hindrance. This is especially true of monks of reputation, who are in great demand for religious performances to receive requisites, etc. As they remain busy with them, they do not get time for meditation.

(iv) Group of students (*gaṇa*) refers to a teacher of Dhamma—one who is busy with teaching work also does not get time for meditation. Therefore students are said to be a source of hindrance.

(v) Work (*kamma*) refers to construction work; such work becomes a constant source of distraction.

(vi) Travel (*addhāna*): Sometimes a monk is required to go to some other place to participate in a religious ceremony, or to receive requisites. The meditator should be free from such duties before taking up meditation.

(vii) Relatives (*ñāti*) refers to illness of one's blood relations, teachers, disciples and fellow-brethren. Their illness becomes a source of distraction. Therefore the meditator has to do his duties to them before taking up meditation.

(viii) Disease (*ābādha*): When suffering from a disease, one has to undergo treatment and get rid of it. Nonetheless, if it is a lingering disease, one may take the risk and devote oneself to meditation.

(ix) Scriptures (*gantha*) are a hindrance to one who is often busy with their study.

(x) Miraculous powers (*iddhi*) are attained at a certain stage of meditation. Interest in them becomes a hindrance to further progress, especially in insight-knowledge (*vipassanā*). Therefore temptation for *iddhi* should be overcome.

In addition to the above, Buddhaghosācariya also refers to what he calls *khuddaka-paḷibodha* or small impediments, such as long hair and nails to be cut, old robes to be mended, and bowls to be cleansed, and so on.

Kalyāṇamitta or the Spiritual Teacher

Kalyāṇamitta literally means a good friend. Here the reference is to a spiritual teacher. After getting rid of all possible hindrances, the prospective meditator should seek out a competent teacher (*ācariya*) who can give him proper guidance.

The Buddha was the noblest friend. Referring to this fact, once the Buddha remarked, "Ānanda, having come to me—the good friend—living beings subject to birth, old age, sickness and death become free from it" (S I 87). Therefore it goes without saying that if the Buddha were living the meditator should go to him. In his absence, the meditator should go to one of the following persons in their descending order: an *arahant*, a non-returner (*anāgāmi*), a once-returner (*sakadāgāmi*), a stream-enterer (*sotāpanna*), a worldling (*puthujjana*) who practises jhāna, a master of the three collections of scriptures (*piṭaka*), a master of two collections, a master of one collection, a master of one section of scriptures with its commentary, and lastly a conscientious teacher (*lajjī*) who has cultivated self-control.

If the meditator finds a competent teacher in his own monastery, well and good. If not, he should go to a monastery where such a teacher resides. Once there, he should not be in a hurry to tell him about the purpose of his coming. He should just keep on doing his duties and wait for a few days. In due course, if the teacher does not ask him about the purpose of his coming, he should find a suitable occasion and tell him about it. He should express his earnestness by telling him that he is ready even to sacrifice his life for the noble cause. When he has thus won his confidence, the teacher is sure to give him a suitable meditation subject with necessary instructions.

Temperament

A meditation subject has to be prescribed for a meditator according to his temperament (*cariyā*). A spiritual teacher who has got the knowledge of reading the thoughts of others (*paracittavijānana-ñāṇa*) can easily ascertain the temperament of a candidate. But one without such knowledge has to keep the candidate under observation for some time and ascertain his temperament before prescribing a suitable meditation subject.

In this connection six temperaments have been mentioned according to the following mental leanings: greed (*rāga*), hate (*dosa*), delusion (*moha*), faith (*saddhā*), intelligence (*buddhi*), and speculation (*vitakka*).

Buddhaghosācariya refers to some teacher who believed in the existence of 14 temperaments—the six basic types and eight others of a mixed character. With reference to this opinion, he says that if temperaments of a mixed character are taken into consideration, there could be many more temperaments.

He also refers to the opinion of some other teachers who believed in the existence of three more temperaments— craving (*taṇhā*), conceit (*māna*), and false view (*diṭṭhi*).

With reference to these, he points out that craving (*taṇhā*) is the same as greed (*rāga*), conceit (*māna*) is closely related to the same. Then again, false view (*diṭṭhi*) does not exist apart from delusion (*moha*). As such, the first two have to be included in the greed temperament, and the last in the delusion temperament respectively. Therefore only the six temperaments given in the beginning have to be treated as basic types.

Though different in nature, some similarity exists between the wholesome and unwholesome temperaments in their mode of expression. For instance, strong faith (*saddhā*) arises in a greed temperament, since greed is strong in nature. Conversely, if among the unwholesome mental states, greed is mild in nature, then among the wholesome mental states faith is mild. Greed keeps on looking for sense-objects, and faith keeps on looking for virtues. Greed does not give up what is harmful, and faith does not give up what is beneficial. Thus they may be said to be parallel in consideration of these points of similarity. In the same way hate (*dosa*) and intelligence (*buddhi*) on the one hand, and delusion and speculation (*vitakka*) on the other have also been compared.

Sources of Temperaments

Initially Buddhaghosācariya refers to two explanations of the unwholesome temperaments given by Upatissa Thera in the *Vimuttimagga*. According to Upatissa Thera, the nature of the first three temperaments is conditioned by the previous lives of the individuals concerned. Thus those who performed good deeds with attachment in their previous lives, and were born in a divine world (*devaloka*), have in their present life a disposition for greed. Those who practised violence in their previous lives, and were born in hells and the Nāga world, have a disposition for hate in the present life. Those who indulged in intoxicating things, and did not care to acquire knowledge, or those who were born among the animals, have delusion in predominance in their present life.

Secondly, Upatissa Thera explains these temperaments on the basis of the predominance of the four elements: earth, water, fire and air. Thus those of a deluded temperament have in their body more of earth and fire, those of a hating temperament have more of water and air, and those of a greedy temperament have all the four elements in equal proportion.

Buddhaghosācariya says that the above two explanations are of a general nature, and as such there is nothing in them to determine the nature of an individual temperament. With these remarks he proceeds to give the orthodox explanation in keeping with the interpretations of the old commentaries.

According to this explanation the different temperaments have been determined according to the nature of rebirth-linking-mind (*paṭisandhi-citta*). Thus those whose actions were mostly motivated by greed, hatred and delusion are born with the respective temperaments. The three wholesome temperaments have to be explained with reference to the respective mental states. As regards those of a mixed character, they have to be accounted for with reference to the mental states concerned. In support of this explanation Buddhaghosācariya quotes at length from an exposition of the topic given in the commentary on the Majjhima Nikāya.

How to Ascertain the Temperaments

The temperaments may be ascertained with reference to five points. They have been stated in the following *gāthā:*

> By the posture, by the action,
> By eating, seeing, and so on,
> By the kind of states occurring,
> May temperament be recognized.[12]

---

12. Translation by Bh. Ñāṇamoli, *The Path of Purification*, III. 87.

(i) Posture (*iriyāpatha*). Walking (*gamana*) of the greed temperament is orderly, that of the hatred temperament is rough, and that of the delusion temperament is disorderly. This explanation has been supported with a quotation from Māgandiya-sutta of Suttanipāta.

The above explanation is more or less true for the remaining three postures also—standing (*ṭhāna*), sitting (*nisajjā*), and lying (*seyyā*). The wholesome temperaments are to be understood more or less in the same way according to their parallel cases.

(ii) Action (*kicca*). The greed temperament does things in a systematic and orderly manner, the hatred temperament does them in a haphazard way, and the delusion temperament does them in an unsystematic and disorderly manner. This has been illustrated with reference to the act of sweeping. In fact, this difference can be observed in all their actions. The wholesome temperaments have to be understood according to their parallel cases.

(iii) Food (*bhojana*). The greed temperament likes soft and sweet food. While taking it, he would relish it. He is pleased to receive some good food. The hatred temperament likes hot and sour things. He would take things in a hurry without relishing them. The delusion temperament (*mohacarita*) has no settled choice. He would take things without paying much attention and besmear his face with them. All the time he would be thinking of this and that.

(iv) Seeing, etc. (*dassanādito*). When the greed temperament happens to see an object even slightly pleasing, he would look at it as if surprised. He would express admiration even for a trivial virtue, and would overlook faults. When the hatred temperament happens to see even a slightly unpleasant object, he would try to avoid it as if tired. He would be irritated even at a trivial fault. He would not recognise even great virtues. The attitude of *mohacarita* towards objects of the above description is indifferent. It is the indifference of the ignorant. He depends on others for his opinion about them. In fact, he repeats what others say. This is true of their reaction to other objects also.

The wholesome temperaments are to be understood with reference to their parallel cases.

(v) Occurrence of mental states (*dhammappavatti*). The explanations given under the four headings above mainly related to the unwholesome temperaments, and the wholesome temperaments were to be understood according to the parallel cases. Under the present heading, all the six basic temperaments are explained individually.

(a) The greed temperament is frequently influenced by the following mental states—deceitfulness, fraud, pride, evil desires, ambition, discontent, self-aggrandisement, and vanity.

(b) The hatred temperament is frequently influenced by the following mental states—anger, enmity, disparaging, domineering, envy and avarice.

(c) The delusion temperament is frequently influenced by the following states—stiffness, torpor, agitation, worry, uncertainty, and holding fast to a certain view.

(d) The faith temperament is frequently influenced by the following states—generosity, desire to see noble ones, desire to listen to religious discourses, joy, ingenuousness, honesty, and trust in things that inspire trust.

(e) The intelligence temperament is frequented by the following states—readiness to be spoken to, possession of good friends, moderation in eating, mindfulness, full awareness, wakefulness, urge for religious life, and exertion.

(f) The speculation temperament is frequented by the following states—talkativeness, sociability, not taking interest in good works, failure to finish undertakings, making plans at night and executing them at day time, and mentally roaming about.

The following meditation subjects have been suggested for the temperaments concerned:

Temperament	**Meditation subject**
greed	ten foulnesses and mindfulness of the body
hatred	four divine abidings and four colour *kasiṇa*
delusion	mindfulness of breathing

faith	six kinds of recollection
intelligence	mindfulness of death, recollection of peace, defining the elements, repulsiveness of food
speculation	mindfulness of breathing

The remaining *kasiṇas* and the four immaterial states (*āruppa*) are suitable for all temperaments.

At the end of the discussion of the temperaments, Buddhaghosācariya says that no explanation of the temperamental types is given in the texts or the commentaries. These explanations are based on the opinions of the teacher. They should, therefore, be treated as so many suggestions for understanding different temperaments.

A Suitable Place

After receiving a meditation subject from the teacher, the meditator has to find out a suitable place for meditation. If it is possible for him to live in the monastery of the teacher, well and good. If not he has to find out a suitable place, not far from that of the teacher, so that he may go to him from time to time for advice.

In this connection Buddhaghosācariya has pointed out the following eighteen monasteries as unsuitable for him: (1) a large monastery where there are many disturbances; (2) a new monastery where construction work is going on; (3) a dilapidated monastery where reparation work is going on; (4) a monastery by the side of a main road, where people may visit day and night; (5) a monastery by the side of a rocky pool, where people often come for water; (6) a monastery close to a place of edible leaves, where people often come to pick them up; (7) a place of flower trees, where people often come for flowers; (8) a place of fruit-bearing trees, where people come for fruits; (9) a famous shrine, where people often come for worship; (10) a monastery close to a city, where people may often assemble; (11) a monastery close to a place of timber trees, where people may come for timber; (12) a monastery surrounded by fields, where disputes may arise; (13) a monastery where there are disagreeable persons; (14) a monastery near a market place, where people assemble from various places for transaction of business; (15) a monastery in a remote area, where people have no faith in religious life; (16) a monastery in a border area which is in dispute; (17) all other places which are likely to create disturbances; and (18) a place where it is not possible to have a spiritual teacher.

> A large abode, a new abode,
> One tumbling down, one near a road,
> One with a pond, or leaves, or flowers
> Or fruits, or one that people seek;
> In cities, among timber, fields,
> Where people quarrel, in a port,
> On border lands, on frontiers,
> Unsuitableness and no good friend—
> These are the eighteen instances
> A wise man needs to recognise
> And give them full as wide a berth
> As any foot-pad hunted road.[13]

Conversely, a place suitable for meditation practices should fulfil the following conditions: (a) neither far from nor too close to the *gocaragāma* (alms resort), and easy of access; (b) not crowded by day, quiet at night; (c) not exposed to mosquitoes, serpents, strong wind and sun; (d) easy to obtain the four requisites; and (e) there are learned and well-disciplined elderly monks whom the meditator may approach from time to time for instructions.

The Earth-Kasiṇa

Having selected a suitable place, the meditator may meditate on a *kasiṇa*-disk (*maṇḍala*), say, of the earth-*kasiṇa*.[14] The earth-*kasiṇa* is said to be of two kinds—made-up (*kata*) and not made-up (*akata*). Directions have been given as to what kind of earth has to be used, in what shape and size the *maṇḍala* has to be prepared. The made-up *maṇḍala* may be fixed at a place (*tatraṭṭhaka*), or portable (*saṃhārima*). The meditator may carry the latter along with him wherever he goes, and concentrate on it according to his convenience.

---

13. Transl. Bh. Ñāṇamoli, *The Path of Purification*, IV. 18.
14. *Kasiṇa* means "wholeness" or "entirety" and this refers to the all-pervading nature of the disk when it has been developed fully. As is said in MN 77.24: "He perceives the earth kasiṇa above, below, around, undivided, measureless."

A disk which is not made up is a natural one, such as a field that has been just ploughed. A meditator with experience of meditation in previous existences can easily obtain *nimitta* on a disk which is not made up. But one without such experience has to have a disk which is made up for his meditation.

Three Kinds of Sign

Here sign (*nimitta*) refers to the object of meditation. There are three kinds of sign: preparatory sign (*parikamma-nimitta*), grasping sign (*uggaha-nimitta*) and counterpart sign (*paṭibhāga-nimitta*).

The preparatory sign (*parikamma-nimitta*) is the actual object selected by the meditator for concentration, such as the earth *kasiṇa* disk in the present case. To begin with, he has to withdraw his mind from all sides and concentrate it on the object.

The grasping image (*uggaha-nimitta*) is the mental image of the object of concentration. While trying to concentrate his mind on the *maṇḍala,* from time to time the meditator has to close his eyes and visualize it. In the course of this practice, a stage comes where he is able to visualize it without the help of the *maṇḍala.* Then the meditator is said to have obtained the *uggaha-nimitta* or the after-image.

The counterpart sign (*paṭibhāga-nimitta*) is the transformed after-image. After obtaining the grasping sign, the meditator develops it further. In the course of continued practice on it, details disappear and the after-image emerges in full brilliance like a looking glass taken out of its case, or a well polished plate made of the mother of pearls, or the disc of the moon just emerged out of a cloud, or the cranes that appear against the back-ground of a rain-cloud.

Access-Concentration and Fixed-Concentration

Concentration is two-fold: access-concentration (*upacāra-samādhi*) and fixed-concentration (*appanā-samādhi*). Access-concentration is so called because it immediately precedes fixed-concentration. This state is attained when the counterpart image (*paṭibhāga-nimitta*) arises. In this state, the five hindrances (*nīvaraṇa*)—sensuous passion, ill-will, sloth and torpor, distraction and worry, perplexity and ignorance—are overcome. But this state of concentration is not steady. It has been compared to a child not yet able to stand steady, but all the time trying to do so.

Appanā is full-fledged concentration or absorption. This ecstatic state is steady. A meditator who attains it is able to remain in it as long as he likes. Therefore it has been compared to a strong man who is able to stand on his legs for a long time. In this state of concentration, not only the five hindrances have been overcome, but the constituents of jhāna—application of mind on the object, sustaining it, rapture, bliss and concentration—also become manifest.

Measures for the Preservation of the Counterpart Image

It is by developing the counterpart sign that the meditator can attain fixed-concentration. It is only after making great efforts that this sign can be obtained. So if fixed-concentration (*appanā*) can be attained immediately, well and good. If not, the counterpart sign must be protected with great care for future development. In this he has to be very particular about the selection of the following conditions:

(i) Abode or *āvāsa*. He has to select an abode whose atmosphere is suitable for meditation practices.
(ii) Alms-resort (*gocara*). It must be at a reasonable distance from the abode.
(iii) Talk (*bhassaṃ*). He must not indulge in any kind of talk likely to lead to the loss of the sign (*nimitta*). In this connection the thirty-two kinds of unsuitable talk (M-a III 233; cf. MN 76.4) and the 10 kinds of suitable talk (MN 24.2) are referred to.
(iv) Person (*puggala*). He should associate with virtuous and pious persons who take interest in the religious life.
(v) Food (*bhojana*). Not all kinds of food are agreeable to every person. Therefore what is agreeable to one must be taken.
(vi) Climate (*utu*). Not every climate suits every person. Therefore the meditator must live in a climate suitable to his constitution.
(vii) Posture or *iriyāpatha*. Among the four postures, what is helpful in keeping with one's concentration should be adopted.

When the meditator develops the counterpart sign (*paṭibhāga-nimitta*) with these safeguards, he may attain fixed-concentration before long. If not, he has to gain further ten-fold skill in fixed-concentration (*appanā-kosalla*):

(i) The body and the personal belongings of the meditator should be kept clean (*vatthu-visadakiriyatā*).

(ii) Equilibrium of the five ethical faculties—faith, energy, mindfulness, concentration, and knowledge—has to be maintained (*indriya-samatta-paṭipādanatā*). When one of them is predominant, others are not able to perform their functions properly. For instance, when faith becomes predominant other faculties become weak in nature. The story of Vakkali Thera has been cited to illustrate the point (SN 22:87). This is generally true of other faculties also. The balance between faith and knowledge on the one hand, and energy and concentration on the other also has to be maintained. Strong mindfulness is desirable, as it functions as the sentinel of the mind.

(iii) Skill in the sign (*nimitta-kosallaṃ*) is needed. It is three-fold: The first refers to skill in obtaining the sign of a *kasiṇa*-disk, etc. The second refers to skill in developing it. The third refers to skill in safe-guarding the same.

(iv) When the mind is slack, it should be roused up by developing the following three factors of enlightenment—investigation of states, energy and rapture. The development of the last three factors—tranquillity, concentration and equanimity—would have the opposite effect. In this connection the Master has said: If a man, who wants to make a small fire, were to put wet cow-dung, grass, sticks, etc., he would not succeed in it. In the same way, when the mind is slack, it could not be roused up by developing the last three factors of enlightenment. On the other hand if the person, who wants to make a fire, were to put dry cow-dung, grass, sticks, etc., he would succeed. In the same way, when the mind is slack, it could be roused up by developing the first three factors of enlightenment.

(v) The mind should be restrained (*niggahetabbaṃ*) when it is necessary to do so. When the mind gets excited due to too much of exertion, it has to be calmed down by development of the following three factors of enlightenment—tranquillity, concentration and equanimity. The development of the three factors of investigation of states, energy and rapture would have the opposite effect. These two cases have been explained with reference to the above two similes used in the reverse order.

(vi) When the mind gets dejected, it has to be gladdened (*sampahaṃsitabbaṃ*). It is when the expected results are not forthcoming that the mind falls into this state. So it has to be encouraged by reviewing the eight conditions for keeping alive a sense of urgency: birth, decay, disease, death, suffering in the states of misery, suffering in the past, suffering in the future, and suffering in the present in seeking for food. Further the mind has to be inspired by contemplating the qualities of the Triple Gem. This practice would keep up the urge for a religious life.

(vii) The mind should be regarded with equanimity (*ajjhupekkhitabbaṃ*) when it is necessary to do so. When the mind is on the right path moving smoothly, the meditator should adopt an attitude of equanimity. He should be like the charioteer who just watches the horses when they are moving smoothly.

(viii) He should not associate with those who are not given to the practice of concentration (*asamāhitapuggala-parivajjanatā*).

(ix) From time to time he should associate with those who are given to such practices (*samāhitapuggala-sevanatā*).

(x) He should have full confidence in the merits of concentration (*tadadhimuttatā*).

After so much of mental training, the meditator may attain fixed-concentration. If not, he should not be disheartened or excited, but should keep up his effort by maintaining mental equilibrium. This has been explained with reference to five beautiful similes:

- a bee, which maintains the balance of its flight, reaches a tree in full bloom, collects honey and enjoys it;
- a medical student, who maintains the balance of his hand, successfully operates upon a lotus leaf and gets through his test;
- a man who maintains the balance of his hand, wraps the cobweb round a stick without breaking it at any place, and receives reward for his dexterity;
- the sailor, who raises or lowers his sail according to the speed of the wind, would reach his destination safely; or
- a student, who would pour oil into a tube without spilling it, would receive reward from his teacher.

In the same way, the meditator who maintains his mental equilibrium and keeps up his effort is sure to attain fixed-concentration in due course.

As a meditator is focussing his attention on the counterpart sign, and fixed-concentration is about to arise, there will be a break in the life-continuum (*bhavaṅga*). Then the mind-door consciousness (*manodvārāvajjana*) will function. Immediately after, there will arise four or five active types of consciousness (*javana-cittāni*). The meditator will attain the fine-material plane (*rūpāvacara-bhūmi*) in relation to the fourth or the fifth type of consciousness. In the former case, the first three types belong to the sensual plane, and in the latter case, the first four belong to it.

The First Jhāna

With the attainment of the fixed-concentration the meditator is said to have obtained the first jhāna. It is free from the five factors (*pañcaṅga-vippahīnaṃ*) called hindrances: sensuous passion, ill-will, sloth and torpor, distraction and worry, and perplexity.

Here it has to be noted that though other unwholesome mental states have not been mentioned, their absence is understood, for no jhāna can be attained when any of the unwholesome states is present. The jhānas of the fine-material plane are attained by transcending the sensual plane. The five hindrances have a special reference to this plane. Therefore they have been specially mentioned in the present case.

The first jhāna is said to be associated with five factors: applied thought (*vitakka*), sustained thought (*vicāra*), rapture (*pīti*), bliss (*sukha*), and concentration (*ekaggatā*). Applied thought (*vitakka*) and sustained thought (*vicāra*) are two states of one and the same process—therefore sometimes one cannot be separated from the other. The fine distinction between the two has been explained with several beautiful similes:

- *vitakka* is like the striking of a bell, and *vicāra* is like the reverberation of the same;
- *vitakka* is like the flapping of wings and taking air by a bird, and *vicāra* is like its smooth movement;
- *vitakka* is like the movement of a bee towards a lotus flower, and *vicāra* is like its hovering over it;

- *vitakka* is like the hand that grasps a dish, and *vicāra* is like the hand that rubs it; or
- *vitakka* is like the pin of the compass set in the centre of a circle, and *vicāra* is like the pin that revolves round it.

Rapture is five-fold: minor rapture (*khuddaka-pīti*), momentary rapture (*khaṇika-pīti*), overwhelming rapture (*okkantika-pīti*), uplifting rapture (*ubbega-pīti*), and pervading rapture (*pharaṇa-pīti*).

The minor rapture is just able to raise the hairs on the body. The momentary rapture just appears and disappears like a flash of lightning. Overwhelming rapture breaks over the body like waves on the sea shore. Uplifting rapture is able to lift one bodily into the air. This has been illustrated by two anecdotes—one of Mahātissa Thera and the other of a girl of the village of Vattakālaka. Pervading rapture suffuses the whole body with a thrilling sensation. In the context of jhāna the last is meant.

The distinction between rapture (*pīti*) and bliss (*sukha*) is also very subtle. One arises when a person obtains a desirable object and the other when it is enjoyed. For instance, when a traveller, exhausted in a desert, happens to hear the sound of water or catches the sight of a wood at some distance, he feels rapture; when he reaches the place and drinks water in the shade, he feels bliss. Where there is rapture there must be bliss, but where there is bliss there may not necessarily be rapture.

The Three Excellences and the Ten Characteristics

Every jhāna—including the first jhāna—has three excellences (*kalyāṇāni*) and ten characteristics (*lakkhaṇāni*). The first excellence is the purity of the path of the jhāna. The second excellence is adopting an attitude of equanimity towards the path that has been treaded. The third excellence is feeling satisfaction at the achievements made so far. The first excellence has three characteristics, the second also has three characteristics, and the third has four characteristics.

As regards the three characteristics of the first excellence, the first is purification of the mind from obstructions to the first jhāna; the second is its movement towards the state of serenity; and the third is the attainment of the same.

As regards the three characteristics of the second excellence, the first is equanimity at the purified mind; the second is equanimity at its movement towards the state of serenity; and the third is equanimity at having attained the same.

As regards the four characteristics of the third excellence, the first is satisfaction at the equilibrium of the mental states; the second is satisfaction at the harmonious function of the faculties; the third is satisfaction at the effective nature of energy; and the fourth is satisfaction at repetition.

Thus there are three excellences and ten characteristics of the first jhāna. This is true of the remaining jhānas also.

The Five Masteries

After attaining the first jhāna the meditator should not be in a hurry to attain the second. In trying to do so, he may even lose what he has already gained. The first jhāna is not yet in a mature state. He has to consolidate what he has achieved before making efforts for further progress. He has to repeat the process, attain the jhāna again and again, and gain proficiency in it. What are known as five masteries (*vasiyo*) have been recommended for that purpose.

(i) The meditator should be able to attend to the jhāna whenever, wherever and for as long as he wishes. This is called mastery of attendance (*āvajjanā-vasī*).

(ii) He should be able to attain it whenever, wherever and as soon as he wishes. This is called mastery of attaining (*samāpajjanā-vasī*).

(iii) He should be able to remain in the jhāna whenever, wherever and for as long as he wishes. This is called mastery of resolving (*adhiṭṭhāna-vasī*).

(iv) He should be able to rise from the jhāna whenever, wherever and as soon as he wishes. This is called the mastery of rising (*uṭṭhāna-vasī*).

(v) He should be able to review the jhāna whenever, wherever and for as long as he wishes. This is called the mastery of reviewing (*paccavekkhaṇā-vasī*).

The Second Jhāna

When the meditator has gained proficiency in the first jhāna he reviews the nature of its factors. *Vitakka* and *vicāra* appear as gross in nature and closer to the sensual plane. He does not feel it safe to be in this state. So he makes efforts for the attainment of the second jhāna. With this object in view, he concentrates on the sign of the earth *kasiṇa* (*pathavī-kasiṇa-nimitta*) and follows the same process as he did in the case of the first jhāna.

Now he attains the second jhāna which is free from two factors—applied thought (*vitakka*), sustained thought (*vicāra*)—and which is associated with three factors—rapture (*pīti*), bliss (*sukha*), and unification (*ekaggatā*). Being free from *vitakka* and *vicāra*, faith or *saddhā* becomes very strong in this jhāna. As a result, the mind becomes more and more tranquil and concentrated.

The Third Jhāna

After rising from the second jhāna the meditator reviews its factors and observes rapture (*pīti*) as gross in nature and the remaining two factors as peaceful. So he concentrates again on the sign of the earth kasiṇa, follows the same method and attains the third jhāna which is free from one factor—rapture—and is associated with two factors—bliss (*sukha*), and unification (*ekaggatā*).

The rapture that the meditator has abandoned is alluring in nature. So he has to be mindful not to be drawn away by it. Then again in this jhāna his mind and body are suffused with bliss (*sukha*). It is also extremely sweet in nature. Still the meditator is able to adopt an attitude of equanimity (*upekkhā*) towards it. For these reasons, this state has been highly praised by the noble ones.

The Fourth Jhāna

After rising from the third jhāna, the meditator observes bliss (*sukha*) also as gross in nature, and equanimity (*upekkhā*) and unification (*ekaggatā*) alone as peaceful. So he concentrates again on the sign of the earth kasiṇa and attains the fourth jhāna which is free from one factor—bliss, and is associated with two factors, equanimity and unification. In this jhāna, equanimity or *upekkhā* appears in its purest form.

This is the explanation of the jhānas according to the four-fold method (*catukka-naya*). According to the five-fold method (*pañcaka-naya*), there are five jhānas. When a meditator who attains the first jhāna observes only applied thought (*vitakka*) as gross in nature, he abandons only applied thought and attains the second jhāna which is associated with four factors. Accordingly the second jhāna of the four-fold method has to be treated as second and third of the five-fold method by dividing its two factors. The third and the fourth jhāna of the first method become the fourth and the fifth of the second method. As regards the first jhāna, there is no change.

SECTION II
The Meditation Subjects

There are forty subjects of concentration meditation (*kammaṭṭhāna*). Except for the earth *kasiṇa*, they have only been referred to above briefly. Here a more detailed explanation of the same is given.

1. The 10 Kasiṇas (Vism V)

The ten *kasiṇa* are (i) earth, (ii) water, (iii) fire, (iv) air, (v) blue, (vi) yellow, (vii) red, (viii) white, (ix) light, and (x) limited space.

(i) The first *kasiṇa*, earth, has already been explained in full. The general details given in it are applicable to all the *kasiṇas*. Therefore in the case of the remaining *kasiṇas*, only their special nature will be mentioned.

(ii) The water-*kasiṇa* is also two-fold: made-up (*kata*) and not made-up (*akata*). A vessel filled with clean water up to the brim belongs to the first category. A pool, lake, lagoon, etc., belong to the second category. A meditator who is new to the practice has to make use of the former. One with previous experience may use the latter.

(iii) The fire-*kasiṇa* is also two-fold: made-up and not made-up. As regards the first, the meditator has to make it in a sheltered place. A piece of cloth or some such thing with a hole in the centre has to be hung in front of it. Then the meditator has to concentrate just on the flame through the hole without paying attention to other details. The second is represented by the flame of a lamp, furnace and so on.

(iv) The *nimitta* of the air-*kasiṇa* is gained in two ways—by sight and by touch. In the first case, it is gained by noticing movement of plants, trees and even the hair of the body. In the second case, it is gained by feeling its touch on one's body.

(v) The blue-*kasiṇa* is also two-fold: made-up and not made-up. The *kasiṇa* is prepared by spreading blue flowers on a casket with petals upwards, or by fastening pieces of blue cloth over the rim of a tray or a casket. A *kasiṇa*-disk (*maṇḍala*) may also be drawn on a wall with blue dye. As regards the second kind, a bush with blue flowers, a blue cloth or gem, etc., can serve the purpose.

(vi-viii) The yellow, red, and white *kasiṇas* have to be understood more or less in the same manner as the blue *kasiṇa*. The only difference is that in preparing these *kasiṇas* the materials of the respective colours have to be used.

(ix) The light-*kasiṇa* is also two-fold: made-up and not made-up. To have the first, a fire may be made in a vessel with a hole in it, and then it be so placed that the light may reflect on the wall through the hole and form a circle. As regards the second, a circle formed on the floor by the sunlight or moonlight passing through a ventilator, has to be treated as such. The former is lasting and the latter is of a short duration.

(x) The limited space-*kasiṇa* is also two-fold: made-up and not made-up. A hole in a wall, an opening in a window, or even a key-hole may represent the former. As regards the latter, a hole made in a cloth, mat, or some such thing may serve the purpose.

2. The 10 Corpse Contemplations (Vism VI)

The ten foulnesses or states of a corpse (*asubhāni*): (i) bloated (*uddhumātakaṃ*), (ii) livid (*vinīlakaṃ*), (iii) festering (*vipubbakaṃ*), (iv) cut-up (*vicchiddakaṃ*), (v) gnawed (*vikkhāyitakaṃ*), (vi) scattered (*vicchiddakaṃ*), (vii) hacked and scattered (*hatavikkhittakaṃ*), (viii) bleeding (*lohitakaṃ*), (ix) worm-infested (*puluvakaṃ*), and (x) skeleton (*aṭṭhikaṃ*).

(i) The bloated corpse, which makes evident how the shape of the body has undergone change, is beneficial to one who has attachment for beautiful shapes.

(ii) The livid corpse, which makes evident how the colour has changed, is beneficial to one who has attachment for complexion.

(iii) The festering corpse, which makes evident the stench of the body, is beneficial to one who has attachment for odours of the body produced by flowers, perfume, etc.

(iv) The cut-up corpse, which makes evident hollowness of the body, is beneficial to one who has attachment for its fullness.
(v) The gnawed corpse, which makes evident the destruction of protrusions of the flesh, is beneficial to one who has attachment for protrusions of flesh at the breasts and similar parts of the body.
(vi) The scattered corpse, which makes evident how the limbs can be scattered, is beneficial to one who has attachment for grace of limbs.
(vii) The hacked and the scattered corpse, which makes evident how the build of the body can be disintegrated, is beneficial to one who has attachment for build of the body.
(viii) The bleeding corpse, which makes evident how a body besmeared with blood can be repulsive, is beneficial to one who has attachment for elegance produced by adornment.
(ix) The worm-infested body, which makes it evident that the body is shared by so many worms, is beneficial to one who owns it with attachment.
(x) The skeleton, which makes evident the repulsive nature of bones, is beneficial to one who has attachment for beautiful teeth.

It is evident from these ten meditation subjects that they are specially meant for those who are of a passionate nature. It is a matter of psychology that for some reason or another a particular feature of the body may have a special attraction for a certain person. The above meditation subjects have been prescribed taking into consideration these psychological types.

3. The 10 Recollections (Vism VII–VIII)

The ten recollections (*anussatī*) on: (i) the Enlightened One (*Buddha*), (ii) the doctrine (*Dhamma*), (iii) the Order of the Noble Disciples (*Saṅgha*), (iv) virtue (*sīla*), (v) generosity (*cāga*), (vi) deities (*devatā*), (vii) death (*maraṇa*), (viii) body (*kāya*), (ix) breathing (*ānāpānasati*), and (x) peace (*upasama*).

(i) The first recollection is on the qualities of the Buddha. This is indicated in the well-known formula: "That Blessed One is such since he is accomplished, fully enlightened, endowed with a clear vision and virtuous conduct, sublime, the knower of the world, the incomparable leader of men to be tamed, teacher of gods and men, enlightened and blessed."

The greatness of the Buddha has to be understood in terms of his enlightenment, his attainments and his position as a supreme teacher. In the formula they have been referred to under ten points.

(ii) The second recollection is on the greatness of the Dhamma. It is given in the following formula: "The Dhamma is well proclaimed by the Blessed One, visible here and now, not delayed, inviting inspection, onward leading, and directly experienceable by the wise." Here the Dhamma has a special reference to the noble path that leads to Nibbāna. It is to be practised by each person for himself or herself, and the results are to be enjoyed immediately in this very life. They have been mentioned in the formula under six points.

(iii) The third recollection is on the greatness of the Saṅgha. This is given in the following formula: "The community of the Blessed One's disciples has entered on the straight path, the community of the Blessed One's disciples has entered on the true path, the community of the Blessed One's disciples has entered on the proper path, that is to say, the four pairs of men, the eight persons; this community of the Blessed One's disciples is fit for gifts, fit for hospitality, fit for offerings, fit for reverential salutation, as an incomparable field of merit for the world."

Here the term Saṅgha refers to the community of the noble ones, who have attained the four supramundane paths (*magga*) and the four supramundane fruits (*phala*). According to the paths and fruits they represent four pairs and eight individual types. These noble ones are worthy of gifts and veneration. The greatness of the Saṅgha has been referred to under nine points in the formula.

The above three recollections are on the Triple Gem. They are of a devotional nature. The first gives an idea of the great teacher, the second gives an idea of the noble path one has to tread, and the third gives an idea of the great disciples who have reached the goal by treading the path.

(iv) The fourth, recollection of virtue, is practised by reflecting on the purity of virtue observed by the meditator without violation.

He notes that it has liberated his mind from so many defilements. As a result, his mind becomes more and more serene, and gradually attains concentration.

(v) The fifth, recollection of generosity, is based on the actual practice of generosity. After due practice, he will enjoy mental freedom as a result of getting rid of avarice, and other unwholesome mental states. This will lead to concentration.

(vi) In practising the sixth, recollection of the devas, the meditator meditates on virtue, knowledge, generosity and understanding whose cultivation leads to birth among the devas. Then he reflects on these noble qualities as present in himself. As he is doing so, his mind becomes more and more serene and attains concentration.

The subjects of these three recollections are supplied by one's own righteous life.

(vii) The seventh recollection, mindfulness of death, has to be practised by contemplating on the inevitable nature of death. To begin with, one should not think of the death of a near and dear one for that would give rise to sorrow; nor should one think of the death of a foe for that would give rise to gladness. One should think of the death of a neutral person. In the light of the same, he should think of the death of others. Then he should think that his own life is subject to the same fate. The nature of death has been explained with reference to eight points.

Attachment to life is very strong. This kind of contemplation will lead to gradual abandonment of the same and other defilements. The mind thus purified will tend towards concentration.

(viii) The eighth recollection, mindfulness of the body, is on the thirty-two parts of the body: hairs of the head, hairs of the body, nails, teeth, skin, muscles, sinews, bones, marrow, kidneys, heart, liver, membranes, spleen, lungs, bowels, intestines, stomach, excrement, brain, bile, digestive juices, pus, blood, grease, fat, tears, sweat, spittle, snot, fluid of the joints and urine. The meditator has to repeat the list of these thirty-two parts loudly both verbally and mentally for a number of times until the image appears.

In the course of this practice, all the parts of the body have to be determined by way of colour, shape, region, locality and delimitation. Further, their five-fold repulsiveness has to be determined by way of colour, shape, smell, origin and locality. The natural colour of the hairs of the head is black. In shape they are long and round like measuring rods. They grow in the upper region. The wet inner skin that envelops the skull is the locality. Delimitation is two-fold: one by like parts and the other by unlike parts. As to the first—delimitation by like parts, the hairs of the head are limited on the inside by the surface of their own roots; on the outside by space; and all round by each other. No two hairs are together. As regards the second—delimitation by unlike parts—the hairs of the head are not the hairs of the body, the hairs of the body are not the hairs of the head. Thus the hairs of the head are not mixed up with the remaining thirty-one parts.

As to the five-fold repulsiveness, if people happen to see something looking like hair in a plate of gruel or rice, they would not like it. In this way, the hairs of the head are repulsive through colour. When people take food at night and feel vegetable fibres having the shape of hair, they become disgusted. Thus hairs are repulsive through shape. When hair is burnt, its smell is disgusting. Thus hairs are repulsive through smell. This repulsiveness is stronger than that of colour and shape. Hairs that grow on pus, blood, urine, dung, bile, phlegm, and the like are repulsive, just as vegetables that grow in a village sewage are repulsive to town-dwellers. This is repulsiveness through origin. Hairs that have grown on the heap of the thirty-one parts of the body are repulsive in nature, just like mushrooms that have arisen on a dung-heap. This is repulsiveness through locality.

This method has to be followed for each of the remaining thirty-one parts also. In due course, when passion and other unwholesome states are overcome, the meditator attains concentration on the *nimitta* of each one of the parts. The meditator who is given to the practice of this meditation is able to conquer both boredom and delight, fear and dread. He can also endure heat, cold and other difficulties.

(ix) Mindfulness of breathing, the ninth recollection, is practised by focussing attention on the breath. The meditator has to begin by counting the in-coming breath and the out-going breath. He should count at least up to five and at most up to ten. When he has been able to concentrate the mind to some extent, he has to dispense with counting, and just follow the course of the breath. If there are physical and mental disturbances, they have to be controlled. Breath has to be regulated until inhalation and exhalation take place smoothly. As he follows the course of breath passing smoothly, it will become subtler and subtler, and a time will come when he will feel as if it is absent. But it is there in a very subtle form. He has to bear this in mind and continue the practice until the counterpart sign (*paṭibhāganimitta*) arises.

(x) The last recollection is on *upasama* or peace that is Nibbāna. The meditator has to contemplate on it as the state free from desire, and the cessation of saṃsāra, the round of rebirths. In this connection he may take help from various epithets, such as the unformed, the truth, the other shore, the deathlessness, the purity and so forth, which have been used in the Suttantas. This kind of contemplation would free the mind from defilements and lead it to concentration.

Upasama is the ultimate goal of the religious life and this contemplation would give the meditator some indirect knowledge of the same. Direct knowledge is only possible with realization, gained by attaining at least the first stage of sainthood.

4. The Four Divine States (Vism IX)

The four divine states are (i) loving-kindness (*mettā*), (ii) compassion (*karuṇā*), (iii) sympathetic joy (*muditā*), and (iv) equanimity (*upekkhā*).

(i) In the first place, loving-kindness has to be developed towards oneself as follows: "May I be happy and free from suffering, may I keep myself free from enmity, affliction and anxiety, and live happily." In the second place, it may be developed towards a near and dear person, like one's preceptor, then towards a neutral person, and last of all towards an enemy, if there is one.

When loving-kindness is practised towards an enemy, thoughts of ill-will may arise. In that case they have to be overcome by training the mind with reference to the following instructions: he should (a) think of the instructions given by the Master in the *Kakacūpama-sutta* (MN 21); (b) think that by harbouring thoughts of ill-will, he would be acting as the enemy wants him to do; (c) think only of the good points of the enemy; (d) think that, since thoughts of ill-will are harmful to himself, they should be treated as inimical; (d) think that all are inheritors of their deeds (*kamma*); (e) think how the Bodhisattva practised loving-kindness during many a birth, (f) think how he was closely related to him in one form or the other in course of saṃsāra, (g) think of eleven benefits of practising loving-kindness as given in the *Mettā-sutta* (AN 11:15); (h) think of the enemy in terms of elements, and (i) exchange gifts with him as a last resort. When the meditator trains his mind according to one or several of these instructions, he is sure to overcome thoughts of ill-will in due course.

He should continue this practice until all the barriers are broken, and he is able to have the same attitude towards persons of all the categories. Further, in the light of the same, he may develop it towards all beings in all the directions. Here it has to be noted that even by developing loving-kindness towards a near and dear one, the meditator may attain concentration.

(ii) In developing compassion (*karuṇā*), it has to be practised towards the following persons in succession: a man in misery, an evil-doer, a happy man who is so because of his good kamma, a near and dear one, a neutral person, and an enemy, if there is one. In case of an enemy, if thoughts of ill-will were to arise, he should overcome them by following the instructions given *vis-à-vis* loving-kindness. Here too, the practice has to be continued to the point of breaking down the barriers between the persons of various categories.

(iii) As regards sympathetic joy (*muditā*), to begin with, it has to be practised towards a companion who is in happy circumstances. Then it has to be practised towards a neutral person and a hostile person successively. In case of the latter, if thoughts of ill-will were to arise, the method recommended in (i) above has to be followed. When the meditator has been able to develop it to the point of breaking down the barriers between persons of various categories, he should suffuse beings in all the directions with the same feeling. The results would again be the same.

(iv) The divine state of equanimity (*upekkhā*) has to be developed only after attaining the third jhāna on the basis of the first three states. In doing so, he has to begin by thinking of the disadvantages of the first three states, and practise equanimity towards a neutral person, a dear person, a boon-companion, and an enemy in succession. When he has been able to have the same attitude towards himself and the rest, he attains the fourth jhāna associated with equanimity and concentration.

5. Perception of Repulsiveness of Food (Vism IX)

There is one perception (*eka-saññā*), namely the perception of repulsiveness of food. The meditator has to develop this perception with reference to the following ten aspects of it: going for it, seeking it, eating, secretion, receptacle, its undigested state, its digested state, its effects, its outflow, and smearing. As the meditator thus concentrates on the repulsive nature of food with reference to these ten aspects, he overcomes greed for tastes, and to the same extent the mind attains concentration. Further it also paves the way for understanding the true nature of the material states.

6. Defining of the Four Elements (Vism IX)

The one defining (*ekavavatthāna*) is the defining of the four elements (*catudhātuvavatthāna*). The defining of the four elements comprises the understanding of the nature of the body in terms of the four elements—earth-element, water-element, fire-element and air-element. It may be practised according to two methods—the short method and the long method. The first is meant for those of sharp intellect and the other for those of slow intellect. According to the first method, the nature of the body has to be understood in terms of the nature of the four elements. According to the second method, the four elements have to be understood in terms of forty-two constituents of the body. Thus the earth-element exists in the body in the form of twenty solid constituents beginning with the hairs of the head and ending with excrement; the water-element exists in the form of twelve watery constituents beginning with bile and ending with urine; the fire-element in the body expresses itself in four ways in the form of heat of warming up, the heat of maturity, the heat of burning up, and the heat of digestion; the air-element expresses itself in six ways in the form of air discharging upwards, discharging downwards, the air in the stomach, the air in the intestines, the air supporting the movement of the limbs and the breath of inhalation and exhalation. Here it has to be noted that the twenty constituents representing the earth-element, and the twelve constituents representing the water-element are the same as the thirty-two parts of the body given in *kāyagatāsati-bhāvanā*. But there the emphasis is on their elemental nature. This meditation serves a double purpose. In the first place, it leads to concentration; and in the second place, it paves the way for understanding the true nature of corporeality.

7. The Four Immaterial States (Vism X)

The thirty-six meditation subjects dealt with so far are related to the four fine-material jhānas (*rūpa-jhāna*), and lead to the attainment of the fine-material plane (*rūpa-bhūmi*). The meditation subjects under discussion here are related to the four immaterial states and lead to the attainment of the immaterial plane (*arūpa-bhūmi*). The former are attained on the basis of material forms and concepts thereof, whereas the latter are attained by transcending them.

There are four immaterial states: (i). sphere of infinite space (*ākāsānañcāyatana*), (ii) sphere of infinite consciousness (*viññāṇa-ñcāyatana*, (iii) sphere of nothingness (*ākiñcaññāyatana*), and (iv) sphere of neither-perception-nor-non-perception (*nevasaññā-nāsaññā-yatana*).

(i) As regards the first immaterial state (*āruppa*), the meditator who has already attained fine-material jhānas, becomes aware of its shortcomings. As a result, he becomes disgusted with the same and aspires after the immaterial state based on boundless space, which appears peaceful to him. With a view to attaining the same, he takes to the practice of meditation on any of the nine *kasiṇas* with the exception of limited space (*paricchin-nākāsa*). When he has been able to attain the fourth fine-material jhāna, he develops the object of the same to infinity. Then he mentally removes the object and observes only unbounded space (*anantākāsa*). The mind attains concentration on the same. The nature of this immaterial state has been referred to in the following words:

"With total overcoming of the perceptions of matter (*rūpasaññānaṃ samatikkamā*), with the disappearance of the reflex-perceptions (*paṭighasaññānaṃ atthaṅgamā*), with non-attention to perceptions of variety (*nānatta-saññānaṃ amanasikārā*), aware of unbounded space (*ananto ākāso ti*), he enters upon and dwells in the state of unbounded space."

Here the expression—perceptions of matter—refers to the perception of the objects of the fine-material plane; the expression—reflex-perceptions—refers to the perceptions that arise as a result of the interaction between the first five sense-organs and their respective objects; and the expression—perception of variety—refers to all those perceptions that take place outside jhānas. Taken together these expressions mean that the first state of the immaterial plane is attained by transcending both the sensual and the fine-material plane.

(ii) After attaining the first immaterial state, the meditator gains proficiency in the same. But soon he discovers that it too is not a safe state, as it is close to the fine-material plane. At the same time he observes that the second state—*viññāṇañcāyatana*—is safer. So he withdraws his mind from the former and applies it to the latter. The mind attains concentration on the same. The first state is now substituted by the infinite consciousness (*ananta-viññāṇa*).

(iii) Here too, after gaining proficiency, the meditator discovers that the very concept of consciousness is a hindrance. At the same time he observes the third state of the sphere of nothingness as safer and develops a sense of voidness. As a result, in due course, a sense of boundless voidness pervades. It substitutes the former, and the mind attains concentration in relation to the same.

(iv) After attaining the third state and gaining proficiency in the same, the meditator discovers that it too is not a safe state as it has been developed in relation to the concept of consciousness. At the same time, he observes that the fourth state of neither-perception-nor-non-perception (*nevasaññānāsaññāyatana*) as safer. Accordingly he directs his mind and attains concentration on it.

In this state the gross forms of perception have subsided and only the subtle ones exist. In this connection, it has to be noted that other associated mental states also exist in a subtle form. But then they are in a subordinate position to subtle perception which exists in a predominant position. For this reason, this immaterial state has been named after it.

Here it has to be noted that in the case of the fine-material jhāna, there is the overcoming of the constituents (*aṅga-samatikka-mana*). Thus when the meditator emerges from the first jhāna and attains the second, he overcomes applied thought (*vitakka*) and sustained thought (*vicāra*). But in the case of the immaterial jhānas (*arūpa-jhāna*), there is the overcoming of the object of meditation (*ālambana-samatikkamana*). Thus it is by overcoming the object of meditation in the fourth fine-material jhāna that the meditator attains the first immaterial state.

As regards constituents (*aṅga*), equanimity and concentration are common to all the four immaterial states, as well as to the last fine-material jhāna. For this reason, in the Abhidhamma where the constituents of jhāna have been taken into consideration, immaterial states have been treated along with the last fine-material jhāna. It has to be borne in mind here that though these two constituents in question are common to all the five jhānas concerned, in the higher states they are subtler than in the lower ones.

The Relation of Meditation Subjects to Different States of Concentration and Jhāna (Vism XI)

Out of the forty meditation subjects, the first thirty-six are based on material forms and objects, whereas the last four are not so based.

Among the two-fold concentration, access-concentration can be attained on all of the forty meditation subjects. But fixed-concentration can be attained only on thirty of them, the ten exceptions being: the first seven and the tenth of the recollections (*anussati*), the perception of the repulsiveness of food, and the defining of the four elements.

As regards the jhānas, all four fine-material jhāna can be attained on the ten *kasiṇa* and mindfulness of breathing (the ninth collection); only the first jhāna can be attained on the ten foulnesses (ten states of a corpse) and mindfulness of the body (the eighth collection); only the first three jhānas can be attained on the first three divine states; and only the fourth jhāna can be attained on the fourth divine state. These differences are explained in terms of the four-fold method of classifying jhāna; the differences according to the five-fold method of classifying jhāna may be understood similarly.

kammaṭṭhāna / *samādhi*	10 *kasiṇa*	10 *asubha*	10 recollections		1–7, 8, 9, 10		4 divine states	1–3, 4	1 food repulsiveness	1 defining elements	4 immaterial states
upacāra	x	x	x	x	x	x	x	x	x	x	x
appanā	x	x		x	x		x	x			x
jhāna 1	x	x		x	x		x				
2	x				x		x				
3	x				x		x				
4	x				x			x			
5–8											x

The first thirty-six meditation subjects lead to the fine-material plane (*rūpa-bhūmi*). The last four meditation subjects, based on unbounded space, unbounded consciousness, nothingness and the subtle perception, lead to the immaterial plane (*arūpa-bhūmi*).

SECTION III
VISM XII–XIII
Benefits of *Samādhi*

The Five Kinds of Super-Normal Power

There are many benefits of practising concentration-meditation. The *Visuddhimagga* refers to five of them. The attainment of the one-pointedness of mind for penetrating into the true nature of things is the most important among them. The meditator who attains the *jhānic* states can also come into the possession of five kinds of super-normal power. These are represented by the five types of higher knowledge (*abhiññā*). These five, plus the knowledge leading to the destruction of defilements (*āsavakkhaya-ñāṇa*), make up the six-fold higher knowledge (*chalabhiññā*). The first five types of knowledge are mundane; the knowledge leading to the destruction of defilements is supramundane.

In the *Visuddhimagga* two chapters—the twelfth and the thirteenth—have been devoted to the explanation of the five kinds of super-normal power represented by the five types of higher knowledge. The twelfth chapter deals with the first knowledge, and the thirteenth chapter with the remaining four. The first knowledge is related to the super-normal powers called *iddhi*. In the *Visuddhimagga* Buddhaghosācariya quotes in full the explanation of ten kinds of *iddhi* given in the Paṭisambhidāmagga. Among them only three represent higher knowledge (*abhiññā*). The remaining seven powers are *iddhi* but not *abhiññā*. For this reason a separate chapter has been devoted to its explanation.

On certain occasions miracles were performed by the Buddha and his disciples for the benefit of others. It is said that the Buddha performed as many as 2509 miracles for the sake of the three Jaṭila-brothers (Vin I 25–34). The twin-miracles performed at Sāvatthī are well-known (Paṭis I 125, Mil 106, Dhp-a III 227). But then it has to be noted in this connection that much importance is not to be attached to them. These powers have no spiritual value. They are the by-products, so to say, of mental development. Attachment to them could be a hindrance to further progress in the religious life. Therefore, according to the Vinaya, performance of miracles is an offence (Vin III 42). All the same, they give evidence of the great mental forces that could be brought into play on attaining the higher levels of mind.

As mentioned above, there are five kinds of super-normal knowledge of the mundane plane that are attained on the basis of jhāna:

(i) the super-normal knowledge within the knowledge of performing miracles (*iddhividha-ñāṇa*).
(ii) the super-normal knowledge of the divine ear (*dibbasota-ñāṇa*).
(iii) the super-normal knowledge penetrating minds (*cetopariya-ñāṇa*).
(iv) the supernormal knowledge of recollecting the previous existences (*pubbenivāsānussati-ñāṇa*).
(v) the super-normal knowledge of passing away and reappearance of beings (*cutūpapāta-ñāṇa*).

(1) *Knowledge of Performing Miracles* (Iddhividha-ñāṇa)

There are ten kinds of *iddhi* or miraculous power:

(i) The miraculous power of the will (*adhiṭṭhānā-iddhi*). It refers to the performance of wonders by exercising will-power.
(ii) The miraculous power of transformation (*vikubbanā iddhi*). By exercising this power, the meditator abandons his natural appearance and assumes the appearance of a boy, a nāga, a supaṇṇa, etc.
(iii) The miraculous power of mind (*manomayā iddhi*). By exercising this power the meditator creates a mental body resembling his physical body in every detail.

These three constitute the first super-normal power (*abhiññā*) called the knowledge of performing miracles (*iddhividha-ñāṇa*).

The remaining kinds of *iddhi* are:

(iv) The miraculous power of knowledge (*ñāṇa-vipphārā iddhi*). It consists in the elimination of unwholesome states through the development of insight knowledge.
(v) The miraculous power of concentration (*samādhi-vipphārā iddhi*). It consists in overcoming the hindrances in the *jhānic* states.
(vi) The miraculous power of the noble ones (*ariyā iddhi*). It refers to the ability of the noble ones to change their attitude at will.

Thus a noble one is able to have an attitude of non-repugnance when there is a situation for repugnance.

(vii) The miraculous power born of kamma (*kammavipākajā iddhi*). It refers to the power of traversing the sky by deities, and so on.

(viii) The miraculous power of a meritorious one (*puññavato iddhi*). It refers to the fortunate position of a universal monarch and a few others endowed with special gifts.

(ix) The miraculous power of the magical arts (*vijjāmayā iddhi*). It refers to the power of the magicians who can travel through the air and do other wonders by their magic.

(x) The miraculous power of right efforts (*sammapayogā iddhi*). In the first place, it refers to the overcoming of the unwholesome states through the cultivation of the wholesome states. In the second place, according to the commentary, it refers to the success attained in arts and sciences.

It is clear from the above account that in the list of *iddhi* all wonders, extra-ordinary powers, natural gifts, worldly success, and magical phenomena have been included. But only the first three *iddhi* constitute the first super-normal power (*abhiññā*) called the knowledge of performing miracles (*iddhividha-ñāṇa*). Among them also the first *iddhi*—the miraculous power of will (*adhiṭṭhānā iddhi*)—has a special significance. Therefore it may be dealt with here at some length. This *iddhi* is eight-fold. It has been presented as follows:

(i) "Being one, he becomes many; having been many, he becomes one." If the meditator wishes to appear in many forms, he should enter into the fourth jhāna, and rising from it should resolve, "May I be a hundred, may I be a hundred." Accordingly he becomes many, like the venerable Cullapanthaka. This method has to be followed in assuming any number of forms.

(ii) "He becomes visible and invisible at will." By exercising this power, a meditator is able to make himself or others visible at a distance, or reveal things which are hidden from sight. Entering into the fourth jhāna, and rising from it he resolves, "May this dark place be lighted up, may this hidden place be revealed." With this resolve it comes to pass.

(iii) "He passes through walls, ramparts and mountains." In this case the meditator enters into the jhāna on space-*kasiṇa*. Rising from it, he adverts to the object—the wall, the rampart or the mountain—to be passed through, and resolves, "Let there be space." It becomes space, and he passes through it unhindered.

(iv) "He dives in and emerges from earth as in water." In this case the meditator enters into jhāna on water-*kasiṇa*. Rising from it, he adverts to the earth and resolves, "Let the earth in such and such area be water." The area so determined turns into water, and he dives in and out.

(v) "He walks on water as on earth." In this case the meditator enters into jhāna on the

(vi) earth-*kasiṇa*. Rising from it, he adverts to water and resolves, "Let the water in such and such area become earth." The area so determined turns into earth, and he walks, stands, sits, or lies down there.

(vii) "Seated cross-legged he travels in space like a winged bird." In this case the meditator enters into jhāna on the earth-*kasiṇa*. Rising from it, he adverts to space and resolves, "Let the space in such and such area be earth." It turns into earth. He travels, stands, sits, and lies down thereon.

(viii) "He touches the sun and moon with hand." Here too the meditator enters into jhāna on a suitable *kasiṇa*. Rising from it he contemplates on the sun or moon and resolves, "Let it be within hand's reach." He finds it so. Then he touches it, sitting or lying down.

(ix) "He controls by means of the body as far as the Brahmā-world." Here, after going through the preliminary stage, if the meditator wishes to go to the Brahmā-world, though it be far, he resolves, "Let it be near." It is near. Though near, he resolves, "Let it be far." It is far. Though many, he resolves, "Let there be few." There are few. If he wishes to go to the Brahmā-world with a visible body, he resolves and directs his mind to accord with his body. When thus resolved and directed, he is suffused with bliss and lightness, and he goes to the Brahmā-world with a visible body. If he wants to go to the Brahmā-world with an invisible body, he resolves and directs his mind to accord with his mind. When thus resolved and directed, he is suffused with bliss and lightness, and goes to the Brahmā-world with an invisible body.

Here it has to be noted that the meditator who wishes to acquire the psychic powers has to attain the eight jhānas on the eight *kasiṇas,* and gain efficiency in the same, in fourteen ways:

(i-iii) He attains the first jhāna on the basis of the eight *kasiṇas* from the earth-*kasiṇa* to white-*kasiṇa* in the direct order, in the reverse order, and in both the direct and reverse order. He repeats it hundreds and thousands of times.

(iv-vi) He attains from the first to the last jhāna, i.e., the base of neither-perception-nor-non-perception (*nevasaññā-nāsaññāyatana*) in the direct order, in the reverse order, and in both the direct and reverse order.

(vii) He attains the first jhāna on earth-*kasiṇa*, the third on the same, then the sphere of infinite space, and then the sphere of nothingness. Thus he omits every second jhāna in the process of attainment.

(viii) He attains the first jhāna on *kasiṇa* omitting every second *kasiṇa.*

(ix) He attains the first jhāna on the earth-*kasiṇa*, the third on the fire-*kasiṇa*; surpassing the blue- *kasiṇa*, he attains the sphere of infinite space; and surpassing the red-*kasiṇa*, he attains the sphere of nothingness. Thus in this case both the jhāna and the *kasiṇa* are omitted alternatively.

(x) He enters into all the jhānas on one and the same *kasiṇa.* Here the difference has to be noted with reference to the various factors of the respective jhāna.

(xi) He attains the first jhāna on different *kasiṇas* one by one. Here the difference has to be noted with reference to the change of the *kasiṇa*-object.

(xii) He attains the eight jhānas in gradual order on the eight *kasiṇas* in the same order. Here the respective jhāna and *kasiṇa* are related in their consecutive order.

(xiii) He determines the number of factors in the jhāna from the first to the last.

(xiv) He determines the nature of the respective objects of the jhāna concerned.

When the meditator has thus trained his mind in the above fourteen ways, and has gained efficiency, he can direct it towards the performance of miraculous power of the will (*adhiṭṭhānā iddhi*).

(2) *Knowledge of the Divine Ear (Dibbasota-ñāṇa)*

It is the celestial beings who are able to listen to sounds at a great distance—with them it is a natural gift. As for the meditator, he has to acquire it. In the beginning, the meditator has to train his ear by listening to various sounds, both gross and subtle. He then develops a mental image of the same as a medium. With this image he attains the fourth jhāna. Rising from it, he develops the capacity of the same by gradual steps until he is able to listen to sounds at thousands of miles away. Thus he exercises the super-normal power of listening to sounds both divine and human, both at a distance and near at hand.

(3) *Knowledge Penetrating Minds (Cetopariya-ñāṇa)*

In this case the meditator has to develop the medium of light with which he will be able to penetrate into the heart-basis, the seat of mind. He observes change of colours of blood taking place therein. It is said that when the mind is joyful, the blood of the heart is red like a ripe banyan fruit; when sad, the blood is black like a jambu fruit; and when the mind is neutral, it is like clean sesame oil. By observing them, he determines the nature of thoughts arising in the mind. By developing the knowledge further he is able to know the nature of other thoughts also without any reference to the heart-basis. These thoughts have been set forth in sixteen forms: thoughts affected and unaffected by greed, affected and unaffected by hate, affected and unaffected by delusion, affected and unaffected by stiffness and torpor, exalted and unexalted, surpassed and unsurpassed, concentrated and unconcentrated, liberated and unliberated. Analytically speaking, these sixteen types cover all the eighty-nine types as given in the Abhidhamma. This super-normal power is also known as the knowledge of reading the thoughts of others (*paracittavijānana-ñāṇa*).

(4) *Knowledge of Recollecting Previous Existences (Pubbenivāsānussati-ñāṇa)*

This is obtained by developing the faculty of memory. In this connection the meditator enters into the four jhāna in due order. Rising from the fourth jhāna, he begins to recollect events of the present life beginning with those of the present moment. When he has been able to remember the events of the present life up to its very beginning, he traces their relation to the previous birth. This process he continues until he is able to recollect many births which are connected by the law of dependent origination (*paṭiccasamuppāda*). This has been set forth in the following words:

> "He directs his mind towards remembering the previous births—one birth, two births, three births ... hundreds of births ... thousands of births ... He remembers that he was born in such and such place in such and such form, and underwent such and such experience. Departing from there, he was born in some other place under different circumstances. Thus he remembers many births with all their special circumstances."

(5) *Knowledge of Passing Away and Reappearance of Beings (Cutūpapāta-ñāṇa)*

This power is acquired by developing the medium of light. Here too, after passing through the preliminary stage and rising from the fourth jhāna, the meditator develops the medium of light to such an extent that even the night would appear as day. Then he perceives beings passing away and being born in happy and miserable places according to their good and bad deeds. For this reason, it is also known as the knowledge of celestial vision (*dibbacakkhu-ñāṇa*). In the discourses of the Buddha this knowledge has been referred to in the following words:

> "With his mind thus concentrated ... he applies and directs his thoughts to the knowledge of the passing away and rebirth of beings. With his divine vision, purified and surpassing human sight, he sees beings passing away and being reborn, low or high, of good or bad appearance, in happy or miserable existences, according to their kamma. He fully realizes that those beings who are given to evil conduct in deed, word and thought, who are revilers of the noble ones, who are of false views, who acquire the kamma of their false views, at the dissolution of body, after death have been reborn in a miserable existence in hell. But those beings who are given to good

conduct in deed, word, and thought, who are not revilers of the noble ones, who are of right views, at the dissolution of body, after death have been reborn in a happy existence in the world of heaven ..."

CHAPTER III

WISDOM (*Paññā*)

VISM XV

SECTION I

The worldling (*puthujjana*) takes things at their face value. As long as this knowledge serves the practical purpose of his day-to-day life, he does not question its validity. With the awakening of critical understanding, it becomes clear that things are not what they appear to be. It is a sense of disillusionment that leads one to enquire into the true nature of things. In other words, it is the experience of suffering (*dukkha*) that urges one to examine the nature of the values of life. As a result, one understands that no phenomenal existence is free from suffering. The present life is not the be-all and end-all of our existence. It is only a drop in the ocean of existence; it is only a stage in the long journey through saṃsāra or the cycle of birth and death.

The immediate cause of suffering is craving (*taṇhā*). The worldling takes the world of appearances, represented by things and beings, as real, treats them as so many permanent entities, and tries to grasp or shun them according to his pleasure or displeasure. In this connection, he performs various activities both good and bad. Thereby he accumulates kamma, which keeps the process of saṃsāra going.

The process of saṃsāra can be put to an end by destroying its cause. It has been mentioned already that craving is the immediate cause of suffering, and for that matter saṃsāra. But then it has to be noted that craving can only exist where there is ignorance (*avijjā*). It is the ignorance of the true nature of things that gives rise to craving. Therefore the destruction of the cause of saṃsāra, in the first instance, means the destruction of ignorance. Opposing this negative aspect of the matter is its positive aspect—the attainment of insight-knowledge. Therefore putting an end to the process of saṃsāra means the cessation of suffering on the one hand and the attainment of the bliss of Nibbāna on the other hand.

In the ultimate analysis, the whole phenomenal existence is represented by so many mental and material states. These have been explained in terms of the five aggregates (*khandha*), twelve sense-bases (*āyatana*), eighteen elements (*dhātu*), twenty-two faculties (*indriya*)[15] and other groups of states (*dhamma*). The states are not independent from one another. They are causally connected according to the law of the dependent origination of things (*paṭicca-samuppāda*).

As stated above, due to misconception, the worldling believes in the existence of beings and things, which he takes as permanent, pleasant and substantial in nature. Hence he develops an attitude of attachment towards them. Once the misconception is removed he perceives only mental and material states brought into existence by certain conditions which are impermanent, painful and unsubstantial in nature. When this insight knowledge is gained, there arises an attitude of detachment towards all composite things. Being free from desire, he will no more accumulate kamma. Consequently, there is an end to the process of saṃsāra. The path to be followed to achieve this purpose is known as the noble eight-fold path.

The above facts have been formulated in what are known as the four noble truths—the truth of suffering (*dukkha-sacca*), the truth of the cause of suffering (*samudaya-sacca*), the truth of the cessation of suffering (*nirodha-sacca*), and the truth of the path leading to the cessation of suffering (*magga-sacca*).

Suffering has been explained in terms of the five aggregates of attachment (*pañcupādānakkhandhā*). Further it can also be explained with reference to the relevant terms of sense-bases (*āyatana*), elements (*dhātu*), faculties (*indriya*) and other groups of states (*dhamma*).

The cause or *samudaya* is generally explained, as already referred to, in terms of craving and ignorance. These two represent only the proximate and remote conditions. Besides these, there are many other conditions that give rise to suffering. They have been

15. Though this group is not exhaustive, it takes into consideration certain states, both mundane and supramundane, which have been analytically stated.

classified into several groups of states (*dhamma*), such as the four floods (*cattāro oghā*), the four fetters (*yoga*), the five hindrances (*nīvaraṇāni*), and so on. In the Abhidhamma they have been explained in terms of so many unwholesome types of thought (*akusala-cittāni*) and mental factors (*cetasikāni*).

Cessation (*nirodha*) is the cessation of suffering. It represents the negative aspect of the *summum bonum*. Nibbāna is the positive aspect, and it is a matter for self-realization. The Path or *magga* is generally known as the Noble Eight-Fold Path. In fact, it refers to all the thirty-seven states that lead to enlightenment (*bodhi-pakkhiya-dhammā*). They have been classified in several groups, such as the four kinds of mindfulness (*cattāro satipaṭṭhānā*), the four kinds of right effort (*cattāro sammappadhānā*), the five ethical faculties (*pañcindriyāni*), and so on.

The path has been explained in several ways. The three-fold training (*sikkhāttaya*) of virtue (*sīla*), concentration (*samādhi*), and wisdom (*paññā*) is the most popular method. The same has been presented in terms of the seven kinds of purification (*satta visuddhi*). Virtue (*sīla*) and concentration (*citta-samādhi*) represent the first two purifications; *paññā* encompasses the remaining five kinds of purification.

In our text the subject-matter has been dealt with in terms of the seven purifications. The first two purifications have been explained in the previous two chapters. In the present chapter, the remaining five are taken into consideration.

As the meditator goes on meditating on the three characteristics (*tilakkhaṇāni*) of the composite things, his insight-knowledge also goes on deepening. As the veils of ignorance are removed one after another, he also goes on gaining light. This phenomenon is indicated by the five kinds of purification and the relevant types of knowledge. When he has attained the fifth purity in order, he may have to face what are known as the ten defilements of insight (*vipassanūpakkilesāni*). But soon he overcomes them and makes further progress. The attainment of the sixth purification is marked by eight moments of knowledge. By the time the meditator attains the eighth moment of knowledge, he is said to have comprehended the true nature of the phenomenal existence. With the attainment of the ninth moment of knowledge, called the knowledge of adaptation (*anuloma-ñāṇa*), he transcends the mundane plane (*lokiya-bhūmi*) and attains the supramundane plane (*lokuttara-bhūmi*).

With the attainment of the first stage of the noble path called *sotāpatti-magga,* he gains the first glimpse of Nibbāna. The meditator is now a noble one or *ariya* destined to attain the final goal (*niyato sambodhiparāyaṇo*). He continues to make further progress till he attains *arahatta,* the last stage of sainthood. By the time he attains the last stage of sainthood, he has fully comprehended suffering (*dukkhaṃ pariññātaṃ*), abandoned the cause of the same (*samudayo pahīno*), realised Nibbāna (*nirodho sacchikato*), and developed the path (*maggo bhāvito*).

Wisdom (*paññā*) is the third and the last stage in the religious life. After undertaking the observance of virtue (*sīla*), the meditator practises concentration (*samādhi*). When the mind is concentrated, he applies it to understanding the true nature of things. Wisdom (*paññā*) has to be understood as distinct from perception (*saññā*) and consciousness (*viññāṇa*). Perception perceives one object as distinct from another in terms of colour, shape, etc. Consciousness is the analytical knowledge. With it we know not only one object as distinct from another, but also its characteristics (*lakkhaṇāni*). Wisdom is intuitional knowledge. With it we know not only the existence of an object and its characteristics, but also the nature of the ultimate reality.

The difference between the three states has been explained with reference to the following analogy. There is a heap of coins lying on the counter of a money-lender. Three persons—a child, a villager and a money-changer—happen to see them. The child only knows their colours and shapes. In addition to this, the villager knows their exchange-value. But he does not know whether they are genuine or not. The money-changer knows all this. He is able to make out a genuine coin from a counterfeit one, by looking at it, or listening to its sound, or smelling it, or tasting it, or weighing it in his hand.

Perception (*saññā*) is like the knowledge of the child, consciousness (*viññāṇa*) is like the knowledge of the villager, and wisdom (*paññā*) is like the knowledge of the money-changer. While the element of knowledge is more or less common to them all, they differ from one another in their nature. Perception can tell us only about the presence of the object. Hence this knowledge is superficial in nature. Consciousness functions in terms of concepts in the intellectual plane. It leads to the knowledge of the three characteristics (*tilakkhaṇāni*) of the composite things. But it does not lead to the attainment of the supramundane path (*lokuttara-magga*). Wisdom, which is critical in nature, leads to the penetration of the true nature of things in the light of the three characteristics, and the attainment of the supramundane path. Thus perception is perceptual, consciousness is conceptual and wisdom is intuitional.

Both perception and consciousness are helpful in attaining wisdom. Therefore it has been said that where there is wisdom, perception and consciousness also exist. But where there is perception and consciousness, wisdom may not exist necessarily.

The Subject Matter of Wisdom

The meditator can realize the true nature of things only through knowledge of the following subjects: 1. aggregates (*khandha*), 2. sense-bases (*āyatana*), 3. elements (*dhātu*), 4. faculties (*indriya*), 5. truths (*sacca*), and 6. dependent origination (*paṭicca-samuppāda*). For this reason, they are also known as the ground or the soil (*bhūmi*) of wisdom (*paññā*). Therefore, before taking on the development of wisdom, the meditator has to have clear knowledge of these subjects.

1. The Aggregates

(Vism XIV)

There are five aggregates: i. the aggregate of form (*rūpa-khandha*), ii. the aggregate of consciousness (*viññāṇa-khandha*), iii. the aggregate of feeling (*vedanā-khandha*), iv. the aggregate of perception (*saññā-khandha*), and v. the aggregate of mental activities (*saṅkhāra-khandha*). The whole phenomenal existence represented by living organisms and inanimate objects can be explained in terms of these five aggregates.

Khandha means a mass or a heap. The five *khandhas* or aggregates are so called because all the states of the respective categories have been included in them. Thus all the material states of past, present and future are included in the aggregate of form or *rūpa-khandha*. This is true of the remaining four aggregates also.

(I) The Aggregate of Form

Rūpa is form or materiality. It is called *rūpa* because it is subject to wear and tear (*ruppana*) because of being affected by heat, cold, etc. There are twenty-eight material qualities, which have been divided into two categories as (a) primary and (b) derived.

(1) The primary material qualities are four in number: earth element, water element, fire element and air element.
(2) The derived material qualities are twenty-four in number: eye, ear, nose, tongue, body, visible datum, sound, odour, flavour, femininity-faculty, masculinity-faculty, life-faculty, heart-basis, bodily intimation, verbal intimation, space element, lightness of matter, malleability of matter, wieldiness of matter, growth of matter, continuity of matter, ageing of matter, impermanence of matter, and physical sustenance.

Buddhaghosācariya has explained these qualities in several ways—from one-fold to ten-fold according to both the Suttantika and Abhidhammika methods. For example, according to the two-fold way of explanation, they are said to be internal and external, gross and subtle, far and near, produced (*nipphanna*) and unproduced (*anipphanna*), sensitive and insensitive, faculty and not-faculty, given rise to by attachment and not given rise to by attachment.

Thus, in this way the five material qualities beginning with the eye are said to be internal because they refer to one's own person, and the rest are external. The twelve material qualities—the nine beginning with the eye and the three elements (excluding the water-element)—are treated as gross because they are impinging in nature; the rest are subtle because they are of the opposite nature. What is subtle is said to be far because it is difficult to perceive, and the rest are near because they are easy to perceive. Eighteen material qualities—the four elements, the thirteen beginning with the eye, and the physical sustenance—are produced, because they manifest in their own nature. The rest, being dependent on them, are said to be unproduced. The five material qualities beginning with eye are said to be sensitive, because they respond to their respective sense data. The sensitive material qualities, together with the three beginning with the femininity-faculty, are faculty in the sense of exercising predominance. The rest are not faculty because they are of the opposite nature. The kamma-born material qualities are said to be given rise to by attachment, and the rest are of the opposite nature.

As regards the three-fold way, they have been explained under the relevant triad-matrix (*tika-mātikā*) of the Dhammasaṅgaṇi. According to the first triad, among the material qualities of an impinging nature, the sense base of form (*rūpāyatana*) is visible, and the remaining are invisible. The subtle material qualities are neither visible nor impinging. The remaining triads have also to be understood in the same way. The five-fold way is based on the causal nature of the material qualities. There are four causes of material qualities: kamma, mind or consciousness (*citta*), temperature (*utu*) and physical sustenance (*āhāra*). The sense faculties and the heartbasis are kamma-born only. The two intimations are consciousness-born only. Sound is born of both consciousness and temperature. Lightness, malleability and wieldiness are born of temperature, consciousness and physical sustenance. All the rest, with the exception of the composite characteristics (*lakkhaṇa-rūpāni*), are born of all four. The composite characteristics do not exist apart from other material states. Therefore their causal nature has not been treated separately.

(II) The Aggregate of Consciousness

To cognize (*vijānāti*) is the characteristic (*lakkhaṇa*) of consciousness (*viññāṇa*). So far as the general nature is concerned, consciousness is treated as one, but it is three-fold from the point of view of its ethical nature—1. wholesome, 2. unwholesome, and 3. indeterminate.

Within this three-fold structure, 89 types of consciousness—21 wholesome types, 12 unwholesome types and 56 indeterminate types (of which 36 are resultants and 20 are inoperative types)—are then expounded as follows:

1. Wholesome consciousness. It is four-fold according to the four planes: (i) sensual, (ii) fine material, (iii) immaterial and (iv) supramundane.
   (i) There are eight types of wholesome consciousness of the sensual plane. Among them, four are associated with joy

(*somanassa*), and four with equanimity (*upekkhā*). Again, four are associated with knowledge (*ñāṇa*) and prompting (*saṅkhāra*), and four are not associated with them.

(ii) There are five types of wholesome consciousness of the finematerial plane according to the five jhānas. The first is associated with the five constituents—applied thought, sustained thought, rapture, bliss and concentration; the second is associated with four, with the exception of sustained thought; the third is associated with three, with the exception of applied thought and sustained thought; the fourth is associated with bliss and concentration; the fifth is associated with equanimity and concentration.

(iii) There are four types of wholesome consciousness of the immaterial plane according to the four immaterial attainments (*aruppāni*). The two constituents—equanimity and concentration—are common to them all.

(iv) There are also four types of wholesome consciousness of the supramundane plane according to the four paths.

So altogether there are twenty-one types of wholesome consciousness.

2. The unwholesome types of consciousness belong to the sensual plane only. There are twelve of them. Among them, eight are rooted in greed (*lobha*), two in hate (*dosa*) and two in delusion (*moha*).

Among the eight rooted in greed, four are associated with joy and four with equanimity; these eight can also be divided into four associated with false view and prompting, and four are not associated with them. Among the two types rooted in hate and associated with resentment (*paṭigha*), one is associated with prompting and the other is not so associated. Among the two types rooted in delusion and associated with equanimity, one is associated with uncertainty and the other with agitation.

3. The indeterminate types of consciousness are of two kinds: (i) the resultant and (ii) the inoperative.

(i) The resultant are of four kinds according to the four planes—(a) the sensual, (b) the fine-material, (c) the immaterial and the (d) supramundane.

(a) Those of the sensual plane are of two kinds—(1) the wholesome and (2) the unwholesome.

(1) The wholesome are of two kinds—those not associated with root-causes (*ahetuka*) and others associated with them (*sahetuka*).

- The wholesome resultants not associated with root causes are of eight kinds: five types represented by eye-consciousness to body-consciousness, mind-element (*mano-dhātu*) with the function of receiving (*sampaṭicchana*) and the two mind-consciousness-elements (*mano-viññāṇa-dhātu*) with the functions of investigation (*santīraṇa*), etc. Among the last two types, one is associated with joy and the other with equanimity.
- The wholesome resultants associated with root-causes are also eight. They correspond to the eight wholesome types.

The associated mental states are the same in both sets. But the resultants are passive like the reflection of a face in a looking-glass, while the wholesome are active like the face itself.

(2) The unwholesome resultants not associated with root-causes (*ahetuka*) are of seven kinds; five types represented by eye-consciousness to body-consciousness, mind-element with the function of receiving, and the mind-consciousness-element with the functions of investigation, etc.

So altogether there are twenty-three resultant types of consciousness of the sensual plane.

(b) There are five resultants of the fine-material plane corresponding to the five wholesome types of consciousness.

(c) There are four resultants of the immaterial plane corresponding to the four wholesome types.

(d) There are four resultants of the supramundane plane corresponding to the four wholesome types.

So in all the four planes, there are thirty-six resultant types of consciousness.

(ii) The inoperative types of consciousness are of three kinds according to the three planes—(a) the sensual, (b) the fine-material and (c) the immaterial. There are no inoperative types in the supramundane plane.

(a) The inoperative types of the sensual plane are of two kinds—those not associated with root-causes (*ahetuka*) and those associated with them (*sahetuka*).

(1) Those not associated with root causes are of two types: mind-element (*mano-dhātu*) and mind-consciousness-element (*mano-viññāṇa-dhātu*). The mind-element performs the function of turning to impressions at the five doors of senses (*pañcadvārāvajjana*). The mind-consciousness-element is of two kinds—one is shared by all and the other is particular to the Arahants. One shared by all is associated with equanimity, and performs the function of turning to impressions at the mind door (*manodvārāvajjana*). The other is associated with joy, and functions when an Arahant gives a smile based on the relevant type of thought (*hasituppāda-citta*). Thus in the sensual plane there are three types of inoperative consciousness not associated with root-causes.

(2) Those associated with root causes are of eight types. They correspond to the eight types of wholesome consciousness.

(b) In the fine-material plane, there are five types of inoperative consciousness corresponding to the five wholesome types.

(c) In the immaterial plane, there are four types corresponding to the four wholesome types.

So in total, there are twenty types of inoperative consciousness.

Thus altogether there are 89 types of consciousness: 21 wholesome types, 12 unwholesome types, 36 resultants and 20 inoperative types.

Fourteen Functions Performed by Eighty-Nine Types of Consciousness

Fourteen functions are performed by 89 types of consciousness: (i) rebirth-linking (*paṭisandhi*), (ii) life continuum (*bhavaṅga*), (iii) turning to impressions (*āvajjana*),[16] (iv) seeing (*dassana*), (v) hearing (*savana*), (vi) smelling (*ghāyana*), (vii) tasting (*sāyana*), (viii) touching (*phusana*), (iv) receiving the impressions (*sampaṭicchana*), (x) investigating them (*santīraṇa*), (xi) determining them (*voṭṭhapana*), (xii) impulsive activity (*javana*), (xiii) registration (*tadālambana*) and (xiv) death (*cuti*).

(i) Rebirth-linking. When beings are born among heavenly and human beings, through the influence of the eight types of wholesome consciousness of the sensual plane, the corresponding eight resultants function in rebirth linking. When a being is born blind, dumb and so on, through the influence of wholesome types of consciousness associated only with two good root-causes, the resultant mind-consciousness-element without any root-cause and associated with equanimity functions in rebirth-linking. These nine types have kamma, sign of kamma (*kamma-nimitta*), or sign of destiny (*gati-nimitta*) as their object at the time of death.

When through the influence of the relevant five types of wholesome consciousness, beings are born in the fine-material plane, the corresponding five resultants function in rebirth-linking. In the same way, when through the influence of the relevant four types of wholesome consciousness, beings are born in the immaterial plane, the corresponding four resultants function in rebirth-linking. These nine types have sign of kamma alone as their object at the time of death.

When, through the influence of the twelve types of unwholesome consciousness, beings are born in a state of misery, the unwholesome resultant mind-consciousness element not associated with any root-cause functions in rebirth-linking. It has kamma, sign of kamma, or the sign of destiny as the object at the time of death.

16. This is two-fold: turning to impressions at the five sense-doors *(pañcadvārāvajjana)* and at the mind-door *(manodvārāvajjana)*.

Thus nineteen types of resultants function in rebirth linking in the three planes—sensual, fine-material and immaterial.

(ii) Life continuum. After the birth of beings, these nineteen types of resultants function as life continuum in the relevant planes and births.

(iii) Turning to impressions. When the living beings are capable of apprehending objects, and when a visual object has come within the range of the eye, there is a disturbance in the life-continuum, and the inoperative mind-element arises, turning at the eye-door. This is true of the next four sense-doors and their objects also. But when any one of the six kinds of sense-objects has come within the range of the mind-door, there is a disturbance in the life-continuum, and the inoperative mind-consciousness element without any root-cause, but associated with equanimity, arises, turning at the mind-door.

(iv-viii) Seeing, hearing, smelling, tasting and touching. When the inoperative mind-element has arisen turning to impressions at the five-sense doors, there arises one of the ten types of resultant consciousness from eye-consciousness to body-consciousness performing the relevant one among the five functions: seeing, hearing, smelling, tasting, and touching.

(ix) Receiving the impressions. After one of the above ten types of consciousness, there arises the mind-element as a wholesome resultant or an unwholesome resultant according to the nature of the preceding type of consciousness, receiving the sense-object concerned.

(x) Investigating. The mind-element is followed by the mind-consciousness-element investigating the same object. Here an unwholesome type is followed by a type of consciousness of the same nature. But with regard to a wholesome type, either it is followed by a wholesome type associated with joy in the case of a desirable object, or one associated with equanimity in the case of a neutral object. This is how the three types of consciousness concerned perform the function of investigating the object.

(xi) Determining. After the investigating consciousness, the inoperative mind-consciousness-element without root-cause, but associated with equanimity, arises, determining the same object.

(xii) Impulsive activity. After the determining consciousness, if the sense-objects are vivid, there arise six or seven impulsive types on the same. In the sensual plane they are among the following 29 types: eight types of wholesome consciousness, twelve types of unwholesome consciousness, and the remaining nine inoperatives. In the case of the sixth sense-door, the same impulsive types arise next to turning to impressions at the mind door.

In the case of the higher planes, the following 26 types arise: the five wholesome types and the five inoperatives of the fine-material plane; the four wholesome types and the four inoperatives of the immaterial plane; the four types of path-consciousness and the four types of fruition-consciousness of the supramundane plane.

So altogether fifty-five types of consciousness—wholesome, unwholesome, inoperative, and resultant—perform the impulsive activities.

(xiii) Registration. At the end of the impulsive activities, in the six sense-doors, if the object concerned is vivid, there arises one of the eleven types of consciousness—eight resultants of the sensual plane associated with root causes, and three resultant mind-consciousness-elements not associated with root-causes—performing the function of registering the impressions.

At the end of registration, the life-continuum resumes its course. When it is interrupted, the same process is repeated according to the conditions concerned.

(xiv) Death. The last moment of a life-time is called *cuti* or death. It takes place in terms of one of the nineteen types that perform rebirth-linking. Thus the process of saṃsāra continues until a being attains emancipation.

(III) The Aggregate of Feeling

All kinds of feeling (*vedanā*) are included in the aggregate of feeling (*vedanā-khandha*). They are of three kinds—wholesome (*kusala*), unwholesome (*akusala*), and indeterminate (*avyākata*). They associate with the relevant types of consciousness. They are also of five kinds—pleasant, painful, joyful, sad and neutral. The first two are physical, and the last three are mental. They are also represented as of six kinds according to the six sense contacts. Every type of consciousness associates with one kind of feeling or the other as the case may be. Therefore, in the Abhidhamma, feeling has been included among those mental factors which are common to all types of thought.

(IV). The Aggregate of Perception

All kinds of perception (*saññā*) are included in the aggregate of perception (*saññā-khandha*). It is also three-fold—wholesome, unwholesome and indeterminate. They associate with the relevant types of consciousness. According to the number of sense-organs, it is also treated as six-fold. There is no type of consciousness that does not associate with perception. For the same reason, it is also treated as of eighty-nine kinds.

(V) The Aggregate of Mental Activities

The aggregate of mental activities or formations (*saṅkhāra*) includes fifty mental states. Together with feeling and perception, which constitute two separate aggregates, they represent fifty-two mental factors (*cetasika*). Formations (*saṅkhāra*) are also of three kinds—wholesome, unwholesome and indeterminate. They associate with the relevant types of consciousness. The term *saṅkhāra* has been used for volition (*cetanā*) in a special sense, for it is volition that plays the leading part in mental activities. For this reason other mental factors, the concomitants of volition, have also been named after it. The volition that associates with the wholesome and unwholesome types of consciousness leads to the accumulation of kamma.

The whole phenomenal existence is represented by three planes—sensual, fine-material and immaterial. All the five aggregates are available in the first two planes, but only the four mental aggregates are available in the immaterial plane. Therefore in the ultimate analysis, phenomenal existence including living beings has to be explained in terms of the five aggregates.

2. Sense Bases

The second way of explaining phenomenal existence is with reference to the twelve sense-bases, *āyatana,* represented by the six sense-organs and the six sense-objects:

1. Eye	7. Visual object
2. Ear	8. Sound
3. Nose	9. Smell
4. Tongue	10. Taste
5. Body	11. Touch
6. Mind	12. Mental object

They are called *āyatana* because they form the bases of their respective types of consciousness and the mental factors. Among them, ten representing the first five sense-organs and their corresponding objects include only material states, which are gross in nature. The base of mind, (*manāyatana*) representing the sixth sense-organ, includes all the eighty-nine types of consciousness. The base of mental states (*dhammāyatana*), representing the sense-object of the mind, includes the material states of a subtle nature, all the fifty-two mental factors and Nibbāna.[17] In other words, all the material states included in the aggregate of form are represented by eleven bases—ten completely and one partially. Three aggregates—feeling, perception and mental activities—are included in the base of mental states (*dhammāyatana*) along with subtle material states and Nibbāna. Content of the base of mind (*manāyatana*) is the same as that of the aggregate of consciousness (*viññāṇa-khandha*). Except for Nibbāna, there is no material difference between the aggregate–group and the sense-base-group. The difference lies only in the arrangement of the mental and material states in the various categories.

3. Elements

The third way of explaining phenomenal existence is with reference to the eighteen elements or *dhātu* represented by the six sense-organs, the six sense-objects and their corresponding types of consciousness.[18]

1. Eye	7. Visual object	13. Visual consciousness
2. Ear	8. Sound	14. Auditory consciousness
3. Nose	9. Smell	15. Nasal consciousness

17. When speaking of the phenomenal existence, Nibbāna included in the twelfth sense-object has to be excluded.
18. Here too, when speaking of the phenomenal existence, Nibbāna included in the twelfth sense-object has to be excluded.

4. Tongue	10. Taste	16. Gustatory consciousness
5. Body	11. Touch	17. Tactual consciousness
6. Mind	12. Mental object	18. Mind consciousness

They are called elements (*dhātu*) because they represent simple mental and material states without any self-substance about them. In this connection it has to be noted that one category of the sense-base-group, namely the base of mind (*manāyatana*), includes all the eighty-nine types of consciousness. In the element-group the 89 types are distributed among seven of the categories, namely nos. 6 & 13–18. The element of mind (*mano-dhātu*) includes three types—turning to impressions at the five sense-doors (*dvārāvajjana*) and the two types of receiving the impressions (*dve sampaṭicchana-cittāni*). Each of the first five element consciousnesses (*viññāṇa-dhātu*)—eye-consciousness to body-consciousness—includes two types each. Thus they represent ten types in all. The element of mind-consciousness (*manoviññāṇa-dhātu*) includes the remaining 76 types.

This separation of the types of consciousness into one category in the sense-base-group, and seven categories in the element-group is the only difference between the two groups. As regards the remaining eleven categories, there is no material difference at all.

4. The Twenty-Two Faculties and the Four Truths

Vism XVI

(I) The Twenty-Two Faculties

In the study of the phenomenal existence and the realization of the ultimate reality, what are known as the twenty-two faculties (*indriyāni*) have also to be taken into consideration. They are so called because they act as the dominating factors in the fulfilment of certain functions.

The first six faculties represent the six sense-organs, which are predominant in their respective spheres. They refer to what is known as internal "self-hood." Femininity and masculinity indicate the two faculties with reference to which the distinction between the two sexes is made. These two faculties are also dependent on the life-faculty which comes next. The five faculties—bodily pleasure, bodily pain, joy, grief and equanimity—represent the feelings that a living being experiences in the course of his journey through saṃsāra. These experiences, in the widest sense, can be interpreted as suffering. The development of the next five ethical faculties—faith, energy, mindfulness, concentration and understanding—leads to the cessation of suffering. The following are the last three faculties: the faculty that "I shall realize what is not yet realized" (*anaññātaññassāmītindriya*), the faculty of partial realization (*aññindriya*), and the faculty of final realization (*aññātāvindriya*). Among them the first faculty is related to the first path stage, the second is related to the next six path and fruition stages, and the third is related to the last fruition stage. Thus the last three faculties belong to the supramundane plane. It is clear from the short account given above that out of the twenty-two faculties, some give rise to the process of saṃsāra and others bring about cessation of the same.

(II) The Four Truths

There are the four truths: suffering, the cause of suffering, the cessation of suffering and the path leading to the cessation of suffering. They are also known as noble truths, because they are understood in full by *ariya* or the noble ones.

The truth of suffering has been presented in terms of birth, ageing, death, sorrow, lamentation, pain, grief, despair, association with undesirable ones, separation from near and dear ones, not getting what one wants, and, in short, the five aggregates of attachment. In the above list, only certain forms of suffering have been given. It is not possible to enumerate all forms of suffering, nor is it necessary to do so. The five aggregates of attachment are the basis of all suffering. The taste of the water in the ocean can be known by taking a single drop of it. In the same way, all forms of suffering can be known in terms of the five aggregates of attachment. For this reason, it has been given as the last item of the list.

The cause of suffering is desire. It is three-fold: craving for sensual pleasures (*kāma-taṇhā*), craving for becoming as represented by fine-material and immaterial forms of existence (*bhava-taṇhā*), and craving for non-becoming (*vibhava-taṇhā*). The first two forms of craving are based on the eternalist view of life, and the last one on the nihilistic view. Craving gives rise to activities which lead to accumulation of kamma that keeps up the process of saṃsāra. An elaborate explanation of this process has been given in the law of the dependent origination of things or *paṭiccasamuppāda*, which has been formulated in terms of twelve constituents.

The truth of the cessation of suffering refers to Nibbāna. It is not a negative state. It does not mean the mere absence of suffering like the absence of a horn on a hare. It is a positive state which is unborn, unbecome, unmade, and unformed. The noble path does not produce it, but leads to its realisation.

The truth of the path leading to the cessation of suffering is represented by eight constituents—right view, right thought, right speech, right action, right livelihood, right effort, right mindfulness and right concentration. Once the right view is gained by understanding the true nature of things, wrong view is abandoned. The development of the remaining seven constituents also leads to the abandoning of the states opposed to them.

Among the eight constituents, right speech, right action and right livelihood represent virtue (*sīla*), the first stage of the noble path; right effort, right mindfulness, and right concentration represent concentration (*samādhi*), the second stage of the path; right view and right thought represent wisdom (*paññā*), the third stage of the path. The fulfilment of virtue leads to the development of concentration, and the latter leads to the attainment of insight-knowledge or *vipassanā-paññā*.

The knowledge of the path is two-fold: one is the second-hand knowledge gained through information, and the other is the first-hand knowledge based on self-experience of penetration into the four truths.

5. Dependent Origination (Vism XVII)

It has been stated above that phenomenal existence can be explained in terms of the mental and material states presented in the three groups—aggregates, sense-bases and elements. These states, as it would appear at first sight, are not independent of one another. They are dependent and inter-related in so many ways. This fact has been explained in the doctrine of the conditional nature of things also called dependent origination or *paṭicca-samuppāda*.

The system of dependent origination of twelve constituents (*dvādasaṅga-paṭiccasamuppāda-naya*), is based on the same principle. It explains the process of saṃsāra in the form of a chain of twelve links: ignorance (*avijjā*)—kamma-formations (*saṅkhārā*)—consciousness (*viññāṇa*)—mentality and materiality (*nāmarūpa*)—the six sense organs (*saḷāyatana*)—contact (*phassa*)—feeling (*vedanā*)—craving (*taṇhā*)—clinging (*upādāna*)—becoming (*bhava*)—birth (*jāti*)—decay and death (*jarāmaraṇa*).

According to this formula from ignorance arise kamma-formations; from kamma-formations arises consciousness; from consciousness arise other mental and physical states; from these mental and physical states arise the six sense organs; from the six sense organs arises contact; from contact arises feeling; from feeling arises craving; from craving arises clinging; from clinging arises becoming; from becoming arises birth, from birth arise decay and death.

Twenty-Four Conditions (Paccaya)

Phenomenal existence and, for that matter, all mental and material states are conditional in nature. Their conditional nature has been explained in terms of the following twenty-four conditions (*paccaya*): root-cause condition (*hetu-paccaya*), object condition (*ārammaṇa-paccaya*), predominance condition (*adhipati-paccaya*), proximity condition (*anantara-paccaya*), contiguity condition (*samanantara-paccaya*), co-nascence condition (*sahajāta-paccaya*), mutuality condition (*aññamañña-paccaya*), support condition (*nissaya-paccaya*), decisive-support condition (*upanissaya-paccaya*), pre-nascence condition (*purejāta-paccaya*), post-nascence condition (*pacchājāta-paccaya*), repetition condition (*āsevana-paccaya*), kamma condition (*kamma-paccaya*), kamma-result condition (*vipāka-paccaya*), sustenance condition (*āhāra-paccaya*), faculty condition (*indriya-paccaya*), jhāna condition (*jhāna-paccaya*), path condition (*magga-paccaya*), association condition (*sampayutta-paccaya*), dissociation condition (*vippayutta-paccaya*), presence condition (*atthi-paccaya*), absence condition (*natthi-paccaya*), disappearance condition (*vigata-paccaya*), and non-disappearance condition (*avigata-paccaya*).

An elaborate explanation of the twenty-four conditions has been given in the Paṭṭhāna, the seventh book of the Abhidhammapiṭaka. They are applicable to the twelve links of the chain of the dependent origination of things. With this general introduction, an explanation of the conditional nature of the individual links in the chain of dependent origination may now be given.

Ignorance (Avijjā)

Avijjā means the ignorance of the four truths and the conditional nature of the five aggregates, in the past, present and future. Ignorance is the veil that conceals the true nature of things. Once it is removed, the truth reveals itself and Nibbāna is attained.

Ignorance is not a kind of first cause like *prakṛiti* of the Sāṅkhya-system. In a chain of events responsible for the rebirth of a living being, it functions as the first condition. In this sense it may be treated as a first cause.

Formations (Saṅkhāra)

The term *saṅkhāra* has been used in several senses. In the widest sense it has been used for all composite things. In the aggregates it has been used as mental activities. Here it has been used in a special sense for those volitions which lead to kamma-formation.

There are twenty-nine volitions of a creative nature: eight related to the wholesome types of consciousness of the sensual plane, twelve related to the unwholesome types of the same plane, five related to the wholesome types of the fine-material plane, and four related to the wholesome types of the immaterial plane.

They have been divided into three categories: meritorious formations (*puññābhisaṅkhāra*), demeritorious formations (*apuññābhisaṅkhāra*), and imperturbable formations (*āneñjābhisaṅkhāra*). The wholesome volitions of the sensual and the fine-material planes belong to the first category, the unwholesome volitions belong to the second category, and wholesome volitions of the immaterial plane belong to the third category.

Volitions express themselves through the three doors of action—body, speech and mind. Accordingly they are known after them also as bodily formations (*kāya-saṅkhāra*), verbal formations (*vacī-saṅkhāra*), and mental formations (*mano-saṅkhāra*). When the eight wholesome volitions and the twelve unwholesome volitions of the sensual plane express themselves through bodily intimation (*kāya-viññatti*), they create bodily formations. When the same volitions express themselves through verbal intimation (*vacī-viññatti*), they create verbal formations. When all the twenty-nine volitions of the three planes occur without any reference to the above two doors, they create mental formations.

One who has not been able to understand the true nature of things, and is labouring under delusion, creates kamma-formations.

The meritorious kamma-formations are conditioned by ignorance (*avijjā*) by way of two *paccaya*: object condition (*ārammaṇa-paccaya*) and decisive support condition (*upanissaya-paccaya*). In the sensual plane, ignorance functions as an object condition when the meditator comprehends ignorance as subject to destruction. In the fine-material plane, it functions so when the meditator reads the thoughts of others with direct knowledge (*abhiññā*). It also functions as a direct support condition in a two-fold way. In the first place, it functions so when a person performs meritorious deeds with a view to overcoming ignorance. In the second place, it functions so when jhānas of the fine-material plane are attained for the same purpose.

The demeritorious kamma-formations are conditioned by ignorance by way of object condition, object predominance condition, object decisive-support condition, decisive-support condition, proximity condition, contiguity condition, proximity decisive-support condition, repetition condition, absence condition, disappearance condition, root-cause condition, co-nascence condition, mutuality condition, support condition, association condition, presence condition, and non-disappearance.

The imperturbable kamma-formations are conditioned by ignorance only by way of decisive support condition.

Consciousness (Viññāṇa)

Here by consciousness or *viññāṇa* are meant the thirty-two resultant types of consciousness. They are conditioned by the three kinds of formation by way of kamma and decisive support condition. Among them the meritorious formations (*puññābhisaṅkhāra*) condition the following twenty-one resultant types of wholesome consciousness: the five resultants beginning with eye-consciousness through to body-consciousness, one kind of mind-element (*mano-dhātu*), two kinds of mind-consciousness-elements (*mano-viññāṇa-dhātu*), eight kinds of wholesome resultants of the sensual plane associated with a root-cause, and five types of resultants of the fine-material plane.

The demeritorious formations condition seven of the resultant types of consciousness: the five unwholesome resultants beginning with eye-consciousness through to body-consciousness, one mind-element and one mind-consciousness-element.

The imperturbable formations condition the four resultant types of consciousness of the immaterial plane.

Thus there are thirty-two resultant types of consciousness conditioned by formations. Among them thirteen—two five-fold consciousnesses (*dvi-pañca-viññāṇa*), two mind-elements and the mind-consciousness-element associated with joy but not with root-cause—function only in the course of existence. The remaining nineteen types function both in rebirth-linking and in the course of existence. In the present context the latter have been taken into special consideration.

Mentality and Materiality (Nāma-Rūpa)

The rebirth-linking consciousness conditions mentality and materiality. By mentality is meant the mental factors represented by feeling (*vedanā*), perception (*saññā*) and formations (*saṅkhāra*). No consciousness arises without the relevant mental factors included in these three aggregates. Here the reference is to the mental factors which associate with the resultant types. Some of them function in rebirth-linking. After the conception of a being, other types of consciousness and the relevant mental factors begin to function. The mental factors in question here are conditioned by resultant types of consciousness in nine ways by way of co-nascence, mutuality, support, association, kamma-result, sustenance, faculty, presence, and non-disappearance.

By materiality is meant corporeality represented by the four primary elements and the derived material states. Among them the heart-basis is conditioned by the types of consciousness concerned in nine ways: by way of co-nascence, mutuality, support, kamma-result, sustenance, faculty, dissociation, presence, and non-disappearance. The other material states are conditioned by them in eight ways: by way of the same conditions with the exception of mutuality.

Six Bases (Saḷāyatana)

The six bases are the six sense-organs. They are conditioned by (i) mentality and (ii) materiality. The mentality is represented by the three aggregates of feeling, perception and formations. The materiality is represented by the four primary elements, the six bases, the life-faculty and sustenance. This conditional nature has got to be understood both individually and collectively.

(i) Mentality as condition. In rebirth-linking the sixth sense-base is conditioned by mentality in seven ways at a minimum: by way of co-nascence, mutuality, support, association, kamma-result, presence and non-disappearance. Some mentality also functions by way of root-cause and sustenance. Accordingly the maximum number of conditions has to be taken into consideration. In the course of existence too, the sixth base is conditioned by the resultant mentality in the same way as explained above. It is also conditioned in six ways at a minimum: by the non-resultant mentality by six of the above conditions except for kamma-result. Here too, the root-cause and sustenance account for the maximum number of conditions.

This explanation has been given with special reference to the conditional nature of the sixth base in the immaterial plane (*arūpa-bhūmi*). In the five-constituent becoming (*pañcavokāra-bhava*), the sixth base is conditioned by the resultant mentality in association with the heart-basis, in the same way as in the case of the immaterial attainments (*aruppāni*). But the first five bases beginning with eye-base are conditioned by it, in association with the four primary elements, by way of co-nascence, support, kamma-result, dissociation, presence, and non-disappearance. Root-cause and sustenance account for the maximum number of conditions.

In the course of the existence of the five-constituent becoming (*pañca-vokāra-bhava*), the resultant sixth base is conditioned by the resultant mentality in seven ways, as above, at a minimum. But the non-resultant part of the sixth base is conditioned by the non-resultant mentality in six ways at a minimum. Here kamma-result is not taken into consideration. The maximum number of conditions has to be accounted for as explained above.

In the course of existence, the five bases beginning with eye are conditioned by the resultant mentality having eye-sensitivity, etc. as their physical base, by way of post-nascence, dissociation, presence, and non-disappearance. The non-resultant mentality has also to be explained in the same way.

(ii) Materiality as condition. As regards materiality, in rebirth-linking the sixth base is conditioned by the heart-basis in six ways by way of co-nascence, mutuality, support, dissociation, presence, and non-disappearance. In rebirth-linking and in the course of existence, the first five sense-bases are conditioned by the four elements in four ways by way of co-nascence, support, presence and non-disappearance. But in rebirth-linking and in the course of existence these five bases are conditioned by the material life-faculty in three ways by way of presence, non-disappearance, and faculty. In the course of existence, sustenance functions in terms of three conditions: presence, non-disappearance, and sustenance. In the course of existence, the sixth base representing the types of consciousness from the visual to the tactual are conditioned by the first five sensebases in six ways by way of support, pre-nascence, faculty, dissociation, presence, and non-disappearance. Again in the course of existence, the sixth base, representing the remaining types of consciousness, is conditioned by the heart-base in five ways by way of support, pre-nascence, dissociation, presence, and non-disappearance.

(iii) Mentality-materiality as condition collectively. In the five-constituent becoming (*pañca-vokāra-bhava*) in rebirth-linking the sixth base is conditioned by mentality with heart-basis (materiality) by way of co-nascence, mutuality, support, kamma-result, association, dissociation, presence, and non-disappearance.

Contact (Phassa)

Contact is six-fold according to the six sense-bases: eye-contact, ear-contact, nose-contact, tongue-contact, body-contact and mind-contact. Contact (*phassa*) is conditioned by the six bases (*saḷāyatana*). Here by *saḷāyatana* are meant the six internal bases, and by *phassa* is meant the contact that associates with the relevant types of consciousness. Two types of resultant consciousness—one wholesome and the other unwholesome—arise in relation to each of the first five bases. Then again, there are twenty-two resultant types of mundane consciousness which arise in relation to the sixth base. They are thirty-two types in all. The contact that associates with these thirty-two types is meant here. According to the types of consciousness, it may also be said to be thirty-two-fold.

The first five sense-bases condition their respective contacts in six ways: by way of support, pre-nascence, faculty, dissociation, presence, and non-disappearance. The mind-base conditions its twenty-two-fold contact in nine ways: by way of co-nascence, mutuality, support, kamma-result, sustenance, faculty, association, presence, and non-disappearance.

Here it has to be noted that the six internal bases function when they come into inter-action with their relevant external bases. Therefore these latter bases also condition the contacts in question. Thus the base of form (*rūpāyatana*) to the base of contact (*phassāyatana*) condition the first five contacts—visual to tactual—in four ways by way of object, pre-nascence, presence, and non-disappearance. All of the six bases condition mind-contact in the same four ways.

Feeling (Vedanā)

Feeling is six-fold according to the six sense-contacts. Feeling is a mental factor that associates with all types of consciousness. Accordingly it is also said to be of eighty-nine kinds. Here only the thirty-two resultant feelings have been taken into consideration. In the five-fold sense-door cognition, the five contacts condition the five kinds of feeling in eight ways: by way of co-nascence, mutuality, support, kamma-result, sustenance, association, presence and non-disappearance. But the resultant feeling associated with receiving, investigation and registration is conditioned by the first five sense-contacts only by way of decisive support. In the mind-door cognition, the mind-contact conditions the resultant feeling, occurring as registration in the above eight ways. This is true of the resultant feeling in the three planes occurring with rebirth-linking, life-continuum, and death. But the feeling associated with mind-door registration is conditioned by mind-contact associated with mind-door adverting only in one way—as decisive support.

Craving (taṇhā)

According to the six sense-objects, craving is also six-fold. Again each is three-fold: craving for sense-desires, craving for becoming and craving for non-becoming. The first is associated with the enjoyment of sense-objects, the second with the eternalist view of things, and the third with the nihilistic view of things. Accordingly, they are of eighteen kinds. According to the internal and external data, their number is thirty-six. In relation to the three periods of time, their number is 108. Here resultant-feeling is taken into consideration. It conditions craving by way of decisive support.

Clinging (Upādāna)

Clinging or grasping is four-fold: clinging to sensuality, false views, rules and vows and a personality as such. Craving conditions clinging to sensuality by way of decisive support. It conditions the remaining three kinds of clinging by way of co-nascence, mutuality, support, association, presence, non-disappearance, root-cause, and decisive-support. When it functions as a decisive support, then it does not function as a co-nascence.

Becoming (Bhava)

Becoming or *bhava* is two-fold: kamma-process becoming (*kamma-bhava*) and rebirth-process becoming (*uppatti-bhava*). The first is the creative process of volitional activities. It is active in nature. The other is the process of the formations of resultants. It is passive in nature.

The second link of the chain, i.e., kamma-formations (*saṅkhāra*), refers only to the creative volitions, whereas kamma-process (*kamma-bhava*) refers to creative volitions and their associated mental states. It could be said that they are two different ways of representing the same thing.

Kamma-bhava is three-fold: meritorious, demeritorious and imperturbable. The first and the third are wholesome in nature, and the second is unwholesome. The resultants so formed or resultant becoming (*vipāka-bhava*), are also three-fold: sensual becoming (*kāma-bhava*), fine-material becoming (*rūpabhava*) and immaterial becoming (*arūpa-bhava*), represented by the relevant aggregates. In sensual becoming and fine-material becoming, (with the exception of worlds of non-perception [*asañña-loka*] which are included in the latter), all the five aggregates are available. (In worlds of non-perception, only the material aggregate is available.) In immaterial becoming the four mental aggregates alone are available.

Clinging conditions two-fold becoming of the fine-material and immaterial planes, and that of the sensual plane as represented by the wholesome actions and results, by way of decisive support. It conditions becoming of the sensual plane as represented by associated unwholesome actions by way of co-nascence, mutuality, support, association, presence, non-disappearance and root-cause. It also conditions becoming of the sensual plane represented by dissociated unwholesome actions by way of decisive support.

Birth (Jāti)

Rebirth of a being depends on the nature of kamma accumulated by him. Therefore birth or *jāti* is said to be conditioned by kamma-process becoming *(kamma-bhava),* which may be either wholesome or unwholesome. This conditional relation is established by way of kamma and decisive support.

Decay and Death (Jarā-Maraṇa)

Birth leads to decay and death by conditioning them by way of decisive support.

The Wheel of Becoming

The twelve constituent dependent origination (*dvādasaṅga-paṭicca-samuppāda*) has also been presented as the wheel of becoming (*bhava-cakka*). The twelve constituents or spokes belong to three periods of time. Thus ignorance and formations belong to the past, the eight beginning with rebirth-linking consciousness belong to the present, and the last two—birth and ageing-and-death—belong to the future.

Between these spokes there are three links (*ti-sandhi*) formed in terms of cause (*hetu*) and fruit (*phala*). Thus between formations and rebirth-linking-consciousness there is the first link in the form of cause-fruit. Between feeling and craving there is the second link in the form of fruit-cause. Between becoming and birth there is the third link in the form of cause-fruit.

They have been further divided into four sections (*catu-saṅkhepā*). Among them ignorance and formations represent the first section; consciousness, mentality-materiality, six-fold base, contact and feeling represent the second; craving, clinging and becoming represent the third; birth, and ageing-and-death represent the fourth.

In fact, the four sections represent five modes each. In the first section with only ignorance and formations, since ignorance leads to craving, craving to clinging and clinging to becoming, there are accordingly five modes in the first section. These five modes represent the kamma-process of becoming in the previous birth (*atīta-kamma-bhava*).

In the second section, the five components are also the five modes: consciousness, mentality-materiality, six-fold base, contact, and feeling. They represent the resultant process of becoming in the present (*vattamāna-vipāka-bhava*).

In the third section, craving, clinging and becoming have been mentioned. But when becoming is mentioned formations are understood. Again when craving and clinging are mentioned, ignorance that associates with them is also understood. Accordingly there are five modes in the third section too. These five modes represent the kamma-process of becoming in the present (*vattamāna-kamma-bhava*).

In the fourth section with birth and ageing-and-death, by "birth" is understood the five modes of consciousness—mentality-materiality, sixfold base, contact and feeling. Ageing-and-death are the decay and death of the same. These five modes represent the resultant process of becoming in future (*anāgata-vipāka-bhava*).

So in these four sections there are twenty modes, which have been represented as the twenty spokes of the wheel of becoming.

There are three rounds in the wheel: the round of kamma (*kamma-vaṭṭa*), which is represented by formations and becoming; the round of defilements (*kilesa-vaṭṭa*), which is represented by ignorance, craving and clinging; and the round of result (*vipāka-vaṭṭa*), which is represented by consciousness, mentality-materiality, the six-fold base, contact and feeling. The wheel of becoming turns on and on in terms of these three rounds as long as the round of defilements (*kilesa-vaṭṭa*) is not cut off.

SECTION II
VISM XVIII
The Seven Purifications

The highest purity (*parama-visuddhi*) is a synonym for Nibbāna. There is a process of purification, marked by seven stages, which leads to the attainment of the same. They are known as seven purifications or *visuddhis*: (1) purification of virtue (*sīla-visuddhi*), (2) purification of mind (*citta-visuddhi*), (3) purification of views (*diṭṭhi–visuddhi*), (4) purification of overcoming of doubts (*kaṅkhā-vitaraṇa-visuddhi*), (5) purification of knowledge and insight into the right and wrong paths (*maggāmagga-ñāṇadassana-visuddhi*), (6) purification of knowledge and insight into practice (*paṭipadā-ñāṇa-dassana-visuddhi*), (7) purification of knowledge and insight into the noble path (*ñāṇadassana visuddhi*).

Purification of virtue (*sīla-visuddhi*) and purification of mind (*citta-visuddhi*) have already been explained in Chapters 1 and 2. The remaining five purifications are attained by understanding the true nature of phenomenal existence on the one hand and that of Nibbāna on the other. In this connection the meditator has to have knowledge of the five aggregates, the twelve bases, the eighteen elements, the twenty-two faculties, the four truths and the law of the dependent origination of things as explained in Section 1 of this chapter. This is the theoretical knowledge of things. It is their practical knowledge that leads to the attainment of the remaining five purifications.

(3) Purification of Views (*diṭṭhi-visuddhi*)

The worldling (*puthujjana*) is deluded by the belief in the existence of an individuality as such (*sakkāya*). But as a matter of fact, this apparent individuality is composed of mental and material states. Through an analytical study, these states can be determined according to their characteristics (*lakkhaṇa*), function (*rasa*), manifestation (*paccupaṭṭhāna*), and the proximate cause (*padaṭṭhāna*).

This practice may be undertaken either on attaining access-concentration (*upacāra-samādhi*) or fixed-concentration (*appanā-samādhi*). One who has attained only the access-concentration may begin with the determination of the four elements and their derivative states. One who has attained a jhāna would emerge from it and contemplate on the mental states, and then on the material states beginning with the heart-basis. One may determine them in terms of 18 elements which are in so many categories; 10½ of these categories include material states only, and 7½ of them include mental states. Another may determine them in terms of 12 bases, which are also in so many categories. Here too 10½ categories include material states, and 1½ categories include mental states. A third may determine them in terms of the five aggregates, which are also in so many categories. The first category includes material states, and the remaining four categories the mental states.

The mental and the material states are interdependent. Just as two sheaves of reeds, propped against each other, stand or fall together, in the same way these states depend on one another.

Here it has to be noted that the mental states to be taken into consideration are the 81 types of mundane consciousness and their associates. The 8 supramundane types of consciousness and their associates are not included among them as they are beyond the knowledge of those who are still in the mundane plane.

As a result of this analysis, the meditator comes to understand that apart from the mental and material states, there is no individual as such. So such expressions as an individual, Deva, Brahmā, etc., are true only in a conventional sense. With this knowledge he attains the purity of views.

(4) Purification through Overcoming of Doubts (*Kaṅkhā-vitaraṇa-visuddhi*)

The meditator understands that the process of mental and material states called a being is not the creation of a causeless cause like a god. They are not without their causes and conditions either. He looks for the causes and conditions within the states themselves and not outside.

This may be understood in several ways:

A meditator may understand the conditional nature of the material states with reference to kamma, consciousness (*citta*), temperature (*utu*) and sustenance (*āhāra*). As regards the mental states, he observes that they come into existence as a result of the inter-relation between the sense-organs and their objects. This is true of all the mental and material states of the three periods of time.

Their conditional nature may also be understood in the reverse order of the terms of the dependent origination of things. Ageing of the states are due to birth, birth is due to becoming ... formations are due to ignorance.

It may be understood in the direct order of the terms also: "Ignorance leads to formations ... birth leads to decay-and-death."

It can also be understood in terms of kamma and result. The past kamma-process-becoming is represented by ignorance, formations, craving, clinging, and becoming. The result of the same appears in the present represented by rebirth-linking-consciousness, mentality-materiality, six-fold sense base, contact and feeling. The present kamma-process is also represented by the same terms as those of the past. The result of the present kamma-process will appear in future as represented by the same terms as those of the present. Thus he understands the conditional nature of mental and material states in the past, present and future. In the light of the same he sees that in fact there is neither a doer of the deeds nor an experiencer of the results. He observes the pure states (*dhamma*) in process: In the past states came into existence due to certain conditions. They ceased giving rise to a new set of states in the present. They too will come to an end giving rise to another set in the future.

When there is a clear understanding of the conditional nature of states in the three periods of time, there is an end to the five kinds of doubt regarding one's past existence—"Was I in the past? Was I not in the past? What was I in the past? How was I in the past? Having been what, what was I in the past?"; the five kinds of doubt regarding one's future existence—"Shall I be in the future? Shall I not be in the future? What shall I be in the future? How shall I be in the future? Having been what, what shall I be in the future?"; and also the six kinds of doubt regarding one's present existence—"Am I? Am I not? What am I? How am I? Whence will this being have come? Whither will it be bound?".

As a result of understanding the conditional nature of things the meditator will be free from these sixteen kinds of doubts. In fact, these sixteen doubts refer to all the sixty-two views. Accordingly the meditator may be said to be free from them to the same extent. This is purification attained by overcoming doubts. It is also known as "knowledge of the relations of states" (*dhammaṭṭhitiñāṇaṃ*), "correct knowledge" (*yathābhūtañāṇaṃ*), and "right vision" (*sammādassanaṃ*).

(5) Purification of Knowledge and Vision of the Right Path and Wrong Path (*Maggāmagga-ñāṇadassana-visuddhi*)

Vism XX

After having a clear conception of the mental and material states along with their relevant conditions, the meditator meditates on their general nature in terms of impermanence (*anicca*), suffering (*dukkha*) and insubstantiality (*anattā*). He does so by way of groups (*kalāpa-sammasana*).

In this connection 24 groups of states (*dhamma*) have been taken into consideration: (i) the states that occur in the doors of consciousness together with the doors and the objects; (ii) the five aggregates; (iii) the six doors; (iv) the six kinds of objects; (v) the six kinds of consciousness (vi) the six contacts; (vii) the six kinds of feeling; (viii) the six kinds of perception; (ix) the six kinds of volition; (x) the six kinds of craving; (xi) the six kinds of applied thought; (xii) the six kinds of sustained thought; (xiii) the six elements; (xiv) the ten *kasiṇa;* (xv) the thirty-two parts of the body; (xvi) the twelve bases; (xvii) the eighteen elements; (xviii) the twenty-two faculties; (xix) the three elements; (xx) the nine kinds of becoming; (xxi) the four jhāna; (xxii) the four measureless states; (xxiii) the four immaterial attainments; and (xxiv) the twelve links of dependent origination.

Further they have to be contemplated upon under forty aspects: as impermanent, as painful, a disease, a boil, a dart, a calamity, an affliction, as alien, as disintegrating, as a plague, a disaster, a terror, a menace, as fickle, perishable, unenduring, as no protection, no shelter, no refuge, as empty, vain, void, not self, as a danger, as subject to change, as having no core, as the root of calamity, as murderous, as due to be annihilated, as subject to cankers, as formed, as Mara's bait, as subject to birth, subject to ageing, subject to illness, subject to death, subject to sorrow, subject to lamentation, subject to despair, and subject to defilement.

Among them ten aspects—as impermanent, as disintegrating, as fickle, as perishable, as unenduring, as subject to change, as having no core, as due to be annihilated, as formed, and as subject to death—refer to impermanence. In this way, contemplation of each aggregate under these ten aspects means fifty kinds of contemplation.

Five aspects—as alien, as empty, as vain, as void, and as not self—refer to insubstantiality. Contemplation of each aggregate under these five aspects means twenty-five contemplations.

The remaining twenty-five aspects refer to suffering. Contemplation of each aggregate under these twenty-five aspects means hundred and twenty-five kinds of contemplation. So altogether there are two hundred kinds of contemplation for each group of *dhamma*.

If the general characteristics are not clear even after this practice, he should concentrate on the mundane composite states with reference to their respective conditions. In this connection he should begin with the material states given rise to by kamma, consciousness, temperature, and sustenance. Next, he should contemplate on the 81 types of consciousness and their associates. In course of this practice, he has to take into consideration how 19 types function as rebirth-linking-consciousness, and how, in course of the life-process, as a result of the interaction between the respective sense-organs, their objects and the presence of other necessary conditions, the remaining types of consciousness come into existence. After due practice of this method, the meditator is sure to have a clear conception of the three characteristics.

Next, he concentrates on the rise (*udaya*) and fall (*vaya*) of the composite states in the three periods of time. He observes that these states come into existence as a result of certain conditions, and attain cessation on the cessation of the same. In this process, nothing comes over from the past to the present, nor does anything go over from the present to the future.

After some practice, what are known as the ten defilements of insight (*vipassanā-upakkilesāni*) arise in him: 1. illumination (*obhāsa*), 2. knowledge (*ñāṇa*), 3. rapture (*pīti*), 4. serenity (*passaddhi*), 5. bliss (*sukha*), 6. resolve (*adhimokkha*), 7. exertion (*paggaha*), 8. assurance (*upaṭṭhāna*), 9. equanimity (*upekkhā*), and 10. attachment (*nikanti*).

At times after the appearance of these phenomena, the meditator begins to labour under the delusion that he has reached the goal. But the well-informed and well-instructed meditator is not deluded by them. He understands that these phenomena are only incidental at this stage. He makes out the path from the not-path, and keeps to the right course.

This is the stage of budding insight (*taruṇa-vipassanā*). By reaching this stage the meditator has made a start in the development of insight (*āraddha-vipassako*).

The Relation of 18 Kinds of Principal Insight-Knowledge (Mahā-vipassanā-ñāṇāni)

The meditator who has gained *sammasana-ñāṇa* (reflective knowledge) is said to have attained the eighteen kinds of principal insight-knowledge in some measure. The eighteen kinds of principal insight-knowledge and the states whose elimination they lead to are as follows:

(i) the contemplation of impermanence leads to the abandoning of the perception of permanence,
(ii) contemplation of pain leads to the abandoning of the perception of pleasure,
(iii) contemplation of not-self leads to the abandoning of the perception of self,
(iv) contemplation of detachment leads to the abandoning of attachment,
(v) contemplation of dispassion leads to the abandoning of delight,
(vi) contemplation of cessation leads to the abandoning of origination,
(vii) contemplation of relinquishment leads to the abandoning of grasping,
(viii) contemplation of destruction leads to the abandoning of the perception of compactness,
(ix) contemplation of the fall of formation leads to the abandoning of the accumulation of kamma,
(x) contemplation of change leads to the abandoning of the perception of lastingness,
(xi) contemplation of signlessness leads to the abandoning of sign,

(xii) contemplation of desirelessness leads to the abandoning of desire,
(xiii) contemplation of voidness leads to the abandoning of the belief in self,
(xiv) development of insight into the phenomenal states that is called higher understanding, leads to the abandoning of clinging to an essence,
(xv) development of correct knowledge and vision leads to the abandoning of misinterpretation due to confusion,
(xvi) contemplation of danger leads to the abandoning of belief due to attachment,
(xvii) contemplation of reflection leads to the abandoning of non-reflection,
(xviii) contemplation of turning away from the round of rebirths leads to the abandoning of conditions conducive to bondage.

The reflective knowledge (*sammasana-ñāṇa*) is represented by the items one to three. Then again, the items eleven to thirteen are the same in meaning. The item fourteen partakes of all kinds of insight. The item fifteen is represented by purification by overcoming doubt. Therefore the meditator who has gained reflective knowledge is said to have attained full knowledge of eight kinds of principal insight, and partial knowledge of the remaining ten kinds. He will be attaining their full knowledge from the knowledge of dissolution (*bhaṅga-ñāṇa*) onwards.

(6) The Knowledge and Vision of the Way (*Paṭipadā-ñāṇadassana-visuddhi*)

Vism XXI

After attaining the purification of the path as distinct from not-path, the meditator tries to attain purification of knowledge and vision of the path. This consists in eight kinds of knowledge, together with the knowledge in conformity with truth as the ninth. They are: (i) knowledge of contemplation of rise and fall (*udayabbayānupassanā-ñāṇa*), (ii) knowledge of contemplation of dissolution (*bhaṅgānupassanā-ñāṇa*), (iii) knowledge of appearance as fear (*bhayatūpaṭṭhāna-ñaṇa*), (iv) knowledge of contemplation of danger (*ādīnavānupassanā-ñāṇa*),

(v) knowledge of contemplation of dispassion (*nibbidānupassanā-ñāṇa*), (vi) knowledge of desire for deliverance (*muñcitukamyatā-ñāṇa*), (vii) knowledge of the contemplation of reflection (*paṭisaṅkhānupassanā-ñāṇa*), (viii) knowledge of equanimity about formations (*saṅkhārupekkhā-ñāṇa*), and (ix) knowledge in conformity with truth (*anuloma-ñāṇa*).

(i) Knowledge of contemplation of rise and fall (*udayabbayānupassanā-ñāṇa*). Being free from the ten defilements referred to above, the meditator further develops his knowledge of rise and fall of the composite states. As a result, their impermanent, painful and unsubstantial nature becomes more and more clear to him. This knowledge free from defilements is also called "insight which has the right course of practice" (*vīthipaṭipanna-vipassanā*).

(ii) Knowledge of contemplation of dissolution (*bhaṅgānupassanā-ñāṇa*). As the meditator goes on meditating on the rise and fall of composite states, a time comes when his mind becomes concentrated on the latter aspect only. He then observes how the composite states break up and are subject to dissolution. Being subject to dissolution, they are impermanent. Now what is impermanent is painful, and what is painful is without any substantiality. So he loses all delight in them. This knowledge gained by reflecting on the perishable nature of the composite things leads to the following advantages: elimination of wrong views regarding becoming, abandoning of craving for life, constant application in what is suitable, purity of livelihood, elimination of anxiety, expulsion of fear, possession of patience and self-control, and overcoming of dissatisfaction.

(iii) Knowledge of appearance as fear (*bhayatūpaṭṭhāna-ñaṇa*). As the meditator concentrates on the perishable nature of things, he sees that all the composite states of the past, in all the three planes of existence, have ceased, those of the present are ceasing, and those of the future will cease. In the light of this knowledge, all these states appear to him as fearful.

(iv) Knowledge of contemplation of danger (*ādīnavānupassanā-ñāṇa*). The meditator, to whom the composite states appear as fearful, does not see any place of security, refuge or protection in the whole phenomenal existence. This understanding of the dangerous nature of the composite states gives him a better knowledge of their three characteristics.

(v) Knowledge of contemplation of dispassion (*nibbidānupassanā-ñāṇa*). When the meditator has seen danger in all composite states, he does not find delight in anything of the three planes of existence. He sees safety and happiness only in dispassion and detachment.

One who sees the fearful nature of the formations (iii above) also sees their danger (iv above). One who sees danger loses all delight in them and develops an attitude of detachment towards them (v). For this reason, as is said in the Paṭisambhidāmagga (Paṭis II 62), they may be treated as three phases of one and the same knowledge.

(vi) Knowledge of desire for deliverance (*muñcitukamyatā-ñāṇa*). As the meditator finds no delight in formations and develops detachment for them, he becomes desirous of being delivered from them. Just like a fish in a net, or a frog in a snake's jaws, he also becomes desirous of being released from these formations. As a result, the knowledge of desire for deliverance arises in him.

(vii) Knowledge of the contemplation of reflection (*paṭisaṅkhānupassanāñāṇa*). When the meditator is desirous of deliverance, he further develops the knowledge of the three characteristics. He contemplates on the formations as impermanent, temporary, limited by rise and fall, disintegrating and perishable. He also sees them as painful because they are oppressing, unbearable, the basis of disease, a calamity, an affliction, a plague, a disaster and so on. They are also without a substance, because they are empty, vain, void, ownerless, and so on. As a result of this contemplation, there arises in him the knowledge of the contemplation of reflection.

(viii) Knowledge of equanimity about formations (*saṅkhārupekkhā-ñāṇa*). As a result of the knowledge of reflective contemplation, the meditator loses the fear of and delight in all formations. He does not find anything to be called "I" or "mine." So he becomes indifferent towards them. With this knowledge of equanimity about formations, the meditator is said to have reached the three-fold door-way leading to Nibbāna. At this stage his mind is directed towards Nibbāna.

The knowledge of desire for deliverance, that of contemplation of reflection and that of equanimity about formations are but three phases of the same knowledge (see Paṭis II 63).

(ix) Knowledge in conformity with truth (*anuloma-ñāṇa*). As the meditator develops the attitude of equanimity towards the composite states, his ethical faculties also become stronger and stronger. In due course he attains the conformity-knowledge. It is so called because on the one hand it conforms to the eight kinds of the preceding knowledge and on the other to the noble path and, for that matter, the fulfilment of the 37 elements of enlightenment. With it, the insight-knowledge (*vipassanā-ñāṇa*), having the formations as their object, reaches the point of culmination. It is the threshold, so to say, of Nibbāna. For this reason, it is also called the culmination of insight-knowledge leading to the noble path (*vuṭṭhānagāminī vipassanā*). But, technically speaking, knowledge in conformity with truth is treated as the last moment in the process (see (7) below).

(7) Purification by Knowledge and Vision (*Ñāṇadassana-visuddhi*)

VISM XXII

After knowledge in conformity with truth (*anuloma-ñāṇa*) there arises maturity-knowledge or *gotrabhū-ñāṇa*. It is so called because at this stage the meditator leaves the lineage of the worldlings (*puthujjana-gotta*) and attains that of the noble ones (*ariya-gotta*). This is an intermediate stage between purification by knowledge and vision of the path, and purification of knowledge and vision. It is still treated as insight because it is in line with it. It has Nibbāna as its object.

The First State of Sainthood

Immediately thereafter follows the first path-knowledge (*magga-ñāṇa*). It performs four functions at one and the same time—it comprehends suffering, abandons the cause of suffering, realises the cessation of suffering, and develops the path that leads to the cessation of suffering. With the attainment of the first path, three of the fetters—delusion of self-hood, doubt about the efficacy of religious life, and belief in rules and vows—are destroyed. It is followed by fruition-knowledge (*phala-ñāṇa*).

The latter is followed by the knowledge of reflection on the path, the fruition, the defilements already eliminated, the defilements yet to be eliminated, and Nibbāna. So there are five kinds of reflective knowledge in the first supramundane state. This is true of the next two kinds of supramundane state also. But after the attainment of the last state, there are no defilements left to be eliminated. Hence only four kinds of reflection are possible here. Therefore there are nineteen kinds of reflection in all the four supramundane states.

The meditator who has attained the first supramundane state is called one who has entered the stream of the noble path or stream-enterer (*sotāpanna*). At the most, he is destined to be born only seven times in the worlds of devas and men (*sattakkhattu-parama*).

The Second State of Sainthood

The meditator, who is now a noble one, follows the same method of meditation, and attains the second state of sainthood, attenuating both sensuous desire and ill-will. He is bound to attain the final emancipation after being born in the sensual plane only once. Therefore he is called once-returner (*sakadāgāmī*).

The Third State of Sainthood

The meditator, who is now a once returner, further follows the same method of meditation, and attains the third state of sainthood by totally destroying the residue of both sensuous desire and ill-will. If he does not attain the final emancipation in this very life, he will be born in a Brahmā-world, where he will attain Nibbāna. As he will not return to the sensuous plane any more, he is called the non-returner (*anāgāmi*).

The Fourth State of Sainthood

The meditator, who is now a non-returner, follows the same method of meditation and attains the fourth and the last state of sainthood, destroying the remaining five fetters: attachment to existence in the fine-material and immaterial planes, conceit, excitement and delusion. He becomes an arahant, a worthy one. In this very life-time he attains the final emancipation of Nibbāna.

Fulfilment of the 37 Elements of Enlightenment

The following are the thirty-seven elements of enlightenment—the four applications of mindfulness (*cattāro satipaṭṭhānā*), the four right efforts (*cattāro sammappadhānā*), the four roads to power (*cattāro iddhipādā*), the five ethical faculties (*pañca indriyāni*), the five mental powers (*pañca balāni*), the seven factors of enlightenment (*satta bojjhaṅgā*), and the eight constituents of the noble path (*aṭṭha maggaṅgāni*).

These thirty-seven elements of enlightenment do not function apart from their associated mental states. Therefore they too have to be understood in relation to these. When the noble path is mentioned, all the thirty seven elements in question are meant. All of these elements associate with every type of consciousness of the first three path-states. As regards the last and the fourth, the four right efforts do not associate with it. When all these elements attain their fulfilment, the meditator gains illumination.

The Destruction of Defilements

It has been already stated how the ten fetters are destroyed by the meditator as he goes on attaining the supramundane paths. Here it has to be noted that, though the ten fetters have been specially mentioned in this connection, the destruction of other defilements too has to be understood in the same way. All these defilements have been classified according to certain principles. Many of the states mentioned in them differ only in form.

They are given here in the order of their destruction by the respective supramundane paths: the ten fetters (*saṃyojanāni*), the ten corruptions (*kilesā*), the ten wrongnesses (*micchattā*), the eight worldly states (*lokadhammā*), the four perversions (*vipallāsā*), the four ties (*ganthā*), the four injustices (*ayatī*), the four cankers (*āsavā*), the four floods (*oghā*), the four bonds (*yogā*), the five hindrances (*nīvaraṇāni*), one adherence (*parāmāso*), the four clingings (*upādānāni*), the four inherent tendencies (*cattāro anusayā*), the three stains (*tīṇi malāni*), the ten unwholesome courses of action (*akusala-kammapathā*), and the twelve unwholesome thought-arisings (*akusala-cittuppādā*).

The ten fetters have been dealt with above. Among the ten corruptions, false view and uncertainty are destroyed by the first path-knowledge; hate is destroyed by the third path-knowledge; greed, delusion, conceit, sloth, agitation, consciencelessness, and shamelessness are destroyed by the fourth path-knowledge.

Among the ten wrongnesses, wrong views, wrong speech (falsehood), wrong action, and wrong livelihood are destroyed by the first path-knowledge; wrong thoughts, malicious speech, and harsh speech are destroyed by the third path-knowledge. Here, only volition is to be understood by speech. Gossip, wrong effort, wrong mindfulness, wrong concentration, wrong deliverance, and wrong knowledge are destroyed by the fourth path-knowledge.

Among the eight worldly states, resentment at loss, misfortune, blame and suffering are destroyed by the third path-knowledge; approval of gain, fortune, praise, and pleasure are destroyed by the fourth path-knowledge.

The five kinds of avarice—avarice about dwellings, families, gain, Dhamma and praise—are destroyed by the first path-knowledge.

Among the three perversions, the perversions of perception, consciousness and views, which find permanence in the impermanent and self in the not-self, and the perversion of view finding pleasure in pain and beauty in the foul are destroyed by the first path knowledge. The perversions of perception and consciousness finding beauty in the foul are destroyed by the third path-knowledge. The perversions of perception and consciousness finding pleasure in the painful are destroyed by the fourth path-knowledge.

Among the four ties, those of adherence to rules and vows and the insistence that "this is the truth," are destroyed by the first path-knowledge; the tie of ill-will is destroyed by the third path-knowledge; and that of covetousness is destroyed by the fourth path-knowledge. The four kinds of injustice based on partiality, ill-will, fear and ignorance are destroyed by the first path-knowledge.

Among the four cankers, that of wrong view is destroyed by the first path-knowledge; that of sensuality is destroyed by the third path-knowledge; those of existence and ignorance are destroyed by the fourth path-knowledge. This is true of the four floods and the four bonds also.

Among the five hindrances, that of uncertainty is destroyed by the first path-knowledge; those of lust, ill-will and worry are destroyed by the third path-knowledge; those of sloth and torpor and agitation are destroyed by the fourth path-knowledge. Adherence (*parāmāsa*) to views, which means holding false views, is destroyed by the first path-knowledge.

Among the four clingings, clinging to views, rules and vows, and to the doctrine of self are destroyed by the first path-knowledge; clinging to existence is destroyed by the fourth path-knowledge.

Among the seven inherent tendencies, wrong views and doubts are destroyed by the first path-knowledge; sensuous passion and hate are destroyed by the third path-knowledge; tendencies of conceit, craving for existence, and ignorance are destroyed by the fourth path-knowledge.

Among the three stains, hate is destroyed by the third path-knowledge; craving and ignorance by the fourth.

Among the ten unwholesome courses of action, killing, stealing, adultery, falsehood and wrong views are destroyed by the first path-knowledge; slandering, harsh words and ill-will are destroyed by the third; frivolous talk and covetousness are destroyed by the fourth.

Among the twelve unwholesome thought-arisings, five—four associated with doubt, and ignorance—are destroyed by the first path-knowledge; two associated with hate by the third; and the remaining five—four dissociated from views and associated with craving, and that associated with distraction and ignorance—are destroyed by the fourth path-knowledge.

Thus on attaining the final enlightenment, all the defilements are destroyed by the four kinds of path knowledge.

Benefits of Wisdom

VISM XXIII

Among others, the following may be mentioned as the benefits of attaining wisdom: (a) destruction of defilements, (b) enjoying the taste of noble fruits, (c) attainment of cessation (*nirodha-samāpatti*), and (d) becoming worthy of receiving gifts and so on.

(i) The destruction of defilements has been explained with reference to the elimination of the ten fetters (*saṃyojanāni*) and the associating mental states. It is the defilements that keep a living being wandering in the ocean of saṃsāra. Therefore destruction of defilements means the cessation of suffering.

(ii) Nibbāna is the object of fruition-states. The noble ones (*ariya*) enjoy the bliss of the same by attaining them. One who attains the first stage of sainthood gains the first vision of Nibbāna. It is gradually developed in the course of attaining the remaining stages. In the last stage, full vision of Nibbāna is gained. The noble ones of the lower stages cannot attain the fruition-states of the higher stages, nor do those of higher stages attain the fruition-states of the lower stages. They attain their respective states only.

(iii) The attainment of cessation (*nirodha-samāpatti*) is so called because both perception (*saññā*) and feeling (*vedanā*) cease in this state. Fruition states can be attained by all noble persons or *ariyas* without any distinction. But the attainment of cessation can be attained only by Arahants, non-returners and those who have already attained all the eight concentration attainments (*samāpatti*), namely, the four form jhānas (*rūpa-jhāna*) and the four immaterial jhānas (*arūpa-jhāna*). The noble ones who attain this state can remain in it even for a week. As the functions of the mind have ceased for the time being, he is not aware even of the existence of his body. It appears that in this state he is wholly absorbed in Nibbāna.

(iv) Having destroyed all defilements and attained the highest state of saint-hood, the noble one becomes worthy of gifts offered and the homage paid by the world.

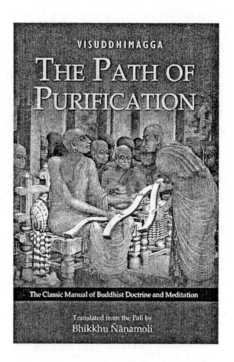